The

High Performing
Woman

52 Take Action Tips for Greater Confidence, Energy & Impact

Dear Angela,
To Your Success!
Susan Treadgold

Susan Treadgold

Sign up for more *Take Action Tuesday* tips at www.TEDlondon.com

Disclaimer

This book introduces the reader to a wide range of general wellness and lifestyle practices. It does not claim to diagnose, treat or cure any medical conditions. This book is not intended to substitute for the services of a trained health care practitioner. Always consult the appropriate doctor or therapist, especially with regards to any symptoms that may require diagnosis and medical attention.

If you choose to apply the ideas and practices contained herein, you are taking responsibility for your actions, risks, and results. The author and its affiliates disclaim all responsibility for any adverse effects that may result directly or indirectly from the information contained in this book.

In other words, please be safe. Use sound judgement and don't do anything silly and hurt yourself. Always consult your doctor(s) or appropriate health professional(s) before engaging in any changes in your health regimen.

First Edition 2018

Kindle e-book ASIN: B0786YY6LG

Published by Susan Treadgold LLC

San Diego, CA

For more information about the author Susan Treadgold, or for coaching or training opportunities, speaking engagements, podcast or media interviews, please visit www.TEDlondon.com or email admin@TEDlondon.com.

This book is dedicated to Cora and Rex.
My favorite girl and my favorite boy in the whole world.

TABLE OF CONTENTS

Endorsements and Accolades 9

Why Did I Write This Book? 13

Why Should You Read This Book? 15

FAQs 17

Chapter 1: Everything is Energy 19

Chapter 2: The Energy Engagement Wheel 21

Chapter 3: InputEnergy 25

Chapter 4: MindEnergy 29

Chapter 5: ConnectionEnergy 33

Chapter 6: PauseEnergy 35

Chapter 7: MoveEnergy 37

Chapter 8: SpaceEnergy 39

Chapter 9: Your Energy Diagnosis 43

Chapter 10: Your Personal Energy Plan 47

Take Action Tip 1: Win Your Morning 49

Take Action Tip 2: Stop Playing It Safe 53

Take Action Tip 3: Improve your Diet 55

Take Action Tip 4: Give Yourself Some Advice 59

Take Action Tip 5: Say "Yes, and…" 61

Take Action tip 6: Be Interested 63

Take Action Tip 7: Reduce Anonymity 65

Take Action Tip 8: Stop Self-Sabotage 69

Take Action Tip 9: Take Off Your Mask 71

Take Action Tip 10: Be Humble 73

Take Action Tip 11: Display Wisdom 75

Take Action Tip 12: Timing is Everything 77

Take Action Tip 13: Have Some Friends - With Benefits . . . 79

Take Action Tip 14: Be Strategic With Your Career 83

Take Action Tip 15: Negotiate 85

Take Action Tip 16: Value the Introverts in Your Life 87

Take Action Tip 17: Stop Letting Others Annoy You 89

Take Action Tip 18: Get to Know Some Inspiring Women . . 91

Take Action Tip 19: Make some Easy Health choices 95

Take Action Tip 20: Measure Your Progress 97

Take Action Tip 21: Be Anything but Average 99

Take Action Tip 22: Bring the Energy 101

Take Action Tip 23: Be Consistent 103

Take Action Tip 24: Build your "No" repertoire 105

Take Action Tip 25: Live like a Centenarian 107

Take Action Tip 26: De-Clutter 109

Take Action Tip 27: Keep a Journal 111

Take Action Tip 28: Develop Your Empathy 113

Take Action Tip 29: Master Game-Changing Events 115

Take Action Tip 30: Get a Green Shot 117

Take Action Tip 31: Develop your Grit 119

Take Action Tip 32: Confidence is Key 121

Take Action Tip 33: Become Self-Aware 125

Take Action Tip 34: Power Up. 127

Take Action Tip 35: Make Space 129

Take Action Tip 36: Be Courageously Authentic 131

Take Action Tip 37: Get Along with People 133

Take Action Tip 38: Get Hydrated 137

Take Action Tip 39: Validate Others 139

Take Action Tip 40: Implement 141

Take Action Tip 41: Keep it Simple 143

Take Action Tip 42: Do a Thought Audit 145

Take Action Tip 43: Be Grateful 147

Take Action Tip 44: Create a "Stop-Doing" list. 149

Take Action Tip 45: Go Slow to Go Fast. 153

Take Action Tip 46: Invest in Yourself 155

Take Action Tip 47: Go to Bed 157

Take Action Tip 48: Eliminate Interference 159

Take Action Tip 49: Be Decisive 161

Take Action Tip 50: Be Directionally Correct 163

Take Action Tip 51: Spend Time on What Matters Most . . . 165

Take Action Tip 51: Create a Confidence Boosting Ritual . . 167

Bonus tip: Pause for Some Quiet 169

About The Author 173

Other Co-Authored Books By Susan Treadgold 175

Hire Susan To Speak at Your Event! 177

The High Performing Woman's Prayer 179

Endorsements and Accolades

A new paradigm of success is being birthed, and Susan Tread-gold is leading the way. As a Holistic Medicine Doctor, I've found that most of our modern health issues are rooted in chronic stress, overwhelm, or burnout. This is because for far too long, our world has sold us an out-of-balanced model of achievement that's based on "hustle," "toughness," and "sacrifice," leading to an epidemic of stress-related illness and burnout. In "The High Performing Woman," Susan shows us a refreshingly NEW model of success and fulfilment, based on joy, wisdom, harmony, and flow. Her "Energy Engagement Wheel" offers a holistic framework for us to cultivate healthier Energy states across all aspects of our lives. The result is a whole new level of high performance, clarity, energy, and enjoyment!

This book may not be massive in its size. But if you choose to implement the Take Action Tips, it can be massive in its impact. Susan is a gifted speaker and coach, and an amazing mother. Most of all, she's a pioneer, sharing a new model of success that our world needs now more than ever.

— **Dr. Edith Ubuntu Chan**,
Holistic Chinese Medicine Doctor, High Performance Coach, Author of #1 Bestselling Book *Super Wellness: Become Your Own Best Healer*. A graduate of Harvard University, Dr. Edith has been featured on CNN, Yoga Journal, Lilou Macé, Juicy Living Tour, Goddess Project Documentary, and more.
www.DrEdithUbuntu.com / www.SuperWellness.com

"I love Susan's Take Action Tips and look forward to receiving them every week. I particularly appreciate her sharing her knowledge of holistic health and strategies for greater mental and physical energy which are also passions of mine. Susan is a gifted coach and inspirational speaker who has inspired both men and women alike."

— Dr. Ben Johnson MD, DO, NMD,
Life Extension and Regenerative Medicine specialist, Minister of Health for the Southern Cherokee Nation RFP, featured in the book and movie *The Secret*, best-selling author of *No Ma'am-ograms! Radical Rethink on Mammograms*, author of *Healing Waters* and co-author of *The Healing Code* and *The Secret of Health: Breast Wisdom*. www.drbenmd.com

"Susan is one of the most talented people I have worked with. Throughout my 20+ year career, I have always looked to mentors and coaches to keep me on the right path, but I have found Susan's advice to be the most helpful. She has an extraordinary ability to hone in on the most important aspects of one's career and skill set and targeting ways of developing them. She is direct and to the point, which I have found refreshing and helpful. Time spent with Susan is a valuable investment and I love her Take Action Tips which help with motivation and momentum."

— Jillian McIntyre
Managing Partner and CEO at 221B Capital LLC

"For me, Susan's Take Action Tips act as an injection of energy and often the motivation and the nudge for action that I really need at a particular time. I like the inspirational quotes and the clarity of suggested numbered actions to take or questions to ponder on. These tips stay with me and I have also found myself filing them away for future reference and

'pick me up' moments. I love that they are now in a book! Thank you, Susan!"

— Viktorija Bird
Director, Global Markets,
Ernst & Young Global Limited

"Susan is a master speaker, and as a coach, she works her magic to help others have lasting impacts."

— Ariane Gorin
President of Expedia Partner Solutions,
board member of Adecco, Advisory Board member
of The Royal Philharmonic Orchestra

"I originally met Susan at a women's networking event. I liked her direct, no-nonsense approach, so the very next day I joined her 21 Day Energy Plan and subscribed to her Take Action Tuesday Tips (TATT). I have seen first -hand how her little nuggets of wisdom can make a huge impact and never more so than this one Take Action Tip from last year. She said: 'You don't have to be perfect, you just have to be directionally correct. Imperfect action trumps perfect procrastination.' It was my 'Aha' moment. I had been working on my website for months feeling like it was never ready or perfect enough so when I read this, I hit the 'Go Live' button there and then. Done, website was LIVE for everyone to see. I won't lie, it was scary, but also very empowering and I wondered why I had waited so long. Subsequently, I have worked with Susan as my business coach—and she is great. She continues to nudge and challenge me out of my comfort zone. I am sure you will enjoy this book of bite-sized wisdom."

— Eloise Mathieu
Gemologist, jewellery designer and founder of
Atelier Eloise www.ateliereloise.com

"Although 'The High Performing Woman: 52 Take Action Tips for Greater Confidence, Energy and Impact' is targeted at the female professional, the concepts are universal. Susan was invaluable in helping me to get perspective on my career, my strengths and weaknesses and my goals. The results have turned out very differently from what I expected and infinitely more worthwhile."

— **Piers D. Butler**
Managing Director, UK Investment bank

"Susan is a mum hero with energy who walks her talk. She is an inspirational speaker and I love her Take Action Tips which give me weekly bursts of motivation. The High Performing Woman (who doesn't want to be one?) provides helpful strategies for more energy and success that you can easily use to take action straight away."

— **Marianna Cherry**
Founder of Mums the Heroes, motivational speaker and author of *50 Colours of Happy and How to Achieve it*

Why Did I Write This Book?

I wrote this book because there is something inside of me that has been waiting far too long to burst forth and make a difference in this lifetime. My vision is to grow more female leaders and to help current female leaders to live their best lives without burning out or opting out. The world will be a better place for everyone with the complementary balance of male and female energy. If you feel the calling to level up, then this book is for you. And for that, you will need to master your physical and mental energy. This will lead to the path of high performance living—the ongoing feeling of full engagement, joy and confidence that comes from consistently living from your best self.

There are two main ways to learn and grow: 1) From experience and 2) by learning from others' experiences. After spending nearly two decades in investment banking and another decade in executive coaching, I have had lots of experience, both good and bad.

I have first-hand knowledge of managing teams *and* mis-managing them; leading and following; being authentic and being someone I wasn't; being clear and lacking direction; being confident and being insecure; thriving and barely surviving; being heard and being ignored; making an impact and making a flop; being energised and being dog-tired; having courage and having to hide; empowering my team and micro-managing; delegating and doing it all to my detriment; being intentional and being reactionary; being organised and being overwhelmed; having a boss as an ally and having a boss as an enemy; being influential and failing to convince; and working on my priorities as well as working all hours of the day on others'. With each of these experiences came valuable learning.

From these experiences, and the wisdom of the many men and women who have inspired me, I know that mastering your physical and mental energy is central to your success. To help you go faster and farther, with more energy, I have distilled the wisdom I've collected into small success habits that you can take action on straight away. This book is comprised of 52 *Take Action Tips* to help *YOU* thrive personally and professionally—and help me stay accountable and "walk the talk"!

WHY SHOULD YOU READ
THIS BOOK?

I HAVE WRITTEN these *Take Action Tips* with you, the profession-al woman, in mind—the one who yearns for holistic success and refuses to accept the notion that personal and professional satis-faction are mutually exclusive. You want more. More success at work. More happiness. More passion in your relationships. More money. More energy. More productivity and more meaning. This book is for you if you'd like to level up and become more focused, productive, in-fluential and successful. These *52 Take Action Tips* are intended to sow the seeds of micro success habits to help women (and men too) achieve greater confidence, energy and impact so they can live the best version of themselves.

More than any time in history, women have the ability today to be, have, and do what they want. Yet we are still facing unequal pay, under-representation in leadership and public office positions, and of-tentimes we still struggle with traditional power dynamics in our in-terpersonal relationships. Instead of voluntarily leaving the workforce, my wish for women is to see them unite together to change workplace policies to enable family life at the same time as earning a living. To thrive personally and professionally; mastering self-leadership as well as leading and inspiring others. This would benefit, of course, both wom-en *and* men. To achieve this, we need to shift the way we think about our energy and power. Everything is energy. And energy is power. The high performing woman recognises that if she takes action to grow and replenish her own energy, she can generate the power to create positive impact in all areas of her personal life, her career and her world. She understands just how much her friends, family and co-workers would benefit from her greater energy and focus.

To combat the common curse of time deficit, each *Take Action Tip* can be read in under one minute. Each contains a digestible shot of wisdom I have collected from personal experience, personal development "gurus," leadership consultants and integrative health & wellness experts. With the encouragement of many from my weekly *Take Action Tuesday Tips* tribe, I have taken the themes from some of my most popular newsletters and have also included a few new ones. So that you can quickly access the relevant micro habits to help you plug up your "energy leaks" and grow your energy awareness, I've categorised the tips into the six areas of my energy wheel: *#MoveEnergy, #MindEnergy, #SpaceEnergy, #InputEnergy, #ConnectionEnergy* and *#PauseEnergy.* I've also noted the high performance habits of *#Clarity, #Energy, #Courage, #Productivity and #Influence.* All in all, 52 bite-sized bits of practical wisdom to spur you on to action so you can create the confidence and energy you need to find and live your purpose, become a high performing woman and make the most of your precious time here on this earth.

FAQs

What is a High Performing Woman?

A High Performing Woman is confident, joyful and fully engaged in her career, relationships and health and has strategies in place for consistently living from her best self.

How should I use this book?

At the bottom of each of the 52 *Take Action Tips* is an action prompt and hashtag reminders of the high performance habits and types of energy that will be developed by the tip.

Read this book chronologically, choose a tip once a week, or go straight to the tips that you think will energise the fastest. Whichever strategy you choose is perfect. Just *take action.*

How can I work with Susan?

Susan has created a series of career masterclasses designed to get you and your team to the next level, faster. She is also a *Certified High Performance Coach* with an advanced curriculum for private individuals as well as groups. Watch for her next De-stress and Assess Retreat and *High Performing Woman group coaching* program!

For more information and to request a client questionnaire, go to www. TEDlondon.com or send an email to admin@TEDlondon.com.

CHAPTER 1

EVERYTHING IS ENERGY

"Everything is energy. Your thought begins it, your emotion amplifies it and your action increases the momentum."

— Unknown

ARE YOU TIRED but wired? Can't get to sleep but can't wake up? Too busy to do what you want yet too busy to even think about what that might be? Overfed and undernourished? Always catching colds? Terrorised by to-do lists? Lacking clarity with your priorities and purpose? Experiencing time poverty? Lacking the courage and confidence to level up in your relationships, health and career? Finding that some tricky characters are stealing your joy? Do you want to positively influence and lead others but struggle with your own self-leadership? If so, then you need to send out an Energy SOS!

The **one single common denominator in lasting success in virtually anything is Energy.** So, knowing where it comes from, where it goes and how to maximise it is the key to success for the high performing woman.

Imagine your body as a big pot and your energy as the water. If you have a full pot of water, you can cook up all sorts of wonderful things in your life. The possibilities are limitless. Allow half of it to drain out and your options become limited. Fail to notice you are nearly on empty (and there will be plenty of signs if you choose to notice) and you can face burnout.

So, what is your energy like now? Let's do an energy check.

Get still and present to how you feel in your mind and body.

Take 3 deep belly breaths.

Now, I'd like you to assess what your energy levels are like right now.

Go ahead and close your eyes. On a scale of 1-10, with one being physically and mentally exhausted and ten being bursting with energy like Tigger from *Winnie the Pooh*. Where are you?

It's all well and good knowing if your energy is low or high, but *real* energy awareness comes from analysing *why* it is low or high and your *preferred* way of topping up your energy pot. The more energy you have, the more results you're able to create—in your relationships, in your career, even in your finances. Imagine what it would be like to operate at a 10/10 every day? Or even one day a week for that matter!

Having worked through this awareness myself and having coached hundreds of busy men and women over the past decade, it became clear to me that there were commonalities in terms of where people get their energy from and, also, where they get their leaks. So, I've developed an *Energy Engagement Wheel* which categorises our energy into six main sources so that you can easily become more energy-aware. This awareness will help you work out how to fill up your "energy pot" and cook up the changes in life that you want.

INCREASE YOUR ENERGY, INCREASE YOUR SUCCESS

"Energy, not time, is the fundamental currency of high performance."

— Jim Loehr

CHAPTER 2

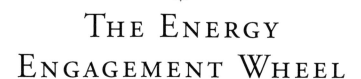

THE ENERGY ENGAGEMENT WHEEL

THE KEY TO SUCCESS IS UNDERSTANDING WHERE YOUR ENERGY COMES FROM, WHERE IT GOES AND HOW TO MAXIMIZE IT

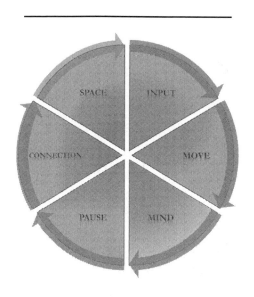

What Is The Energy Engagement Wheel?

T HE Energy Engagement Wheel provides a visual depiction of how your vitality comes from proactively engaging with our six main energy sources: InputEnergy, MoveEnergy, MindEnergy, PauseEnergy, ConnectionEnergy and SpaceEnergy. We all tend to have areas of strength and most of us also have an energy "leak" somewhere! Getting clarity on what is energizing and de-energizing us is the first step towards becoming a High Performing Woman.

How Do I Use The Energy Wheel?

Bringing awareness to the source of your vibrancy or depletion helps you proactively manage your energy. To use this diagnostic model, just scribble down a circle on a sheet of paper and copy the six pie slices above to track your energy on a weekly basis.

To plot your energy, use a scale of 0-10. A score of zero means you are getting no energy from that specific pie slice (i.e., the source of a big energy "leak"). A score of 10 means your energy from that pie slice (e.g., Mind, Move, etc.) could not be better.

Use the epicenter of the wheel for a score of zero and the outer perimeter of each pie slice as ten each. E.g., if your MindEnergy is 5/10, plot a dot halfway up the imaginary spoke in the pie slice.

Before doing this, please read a description of each energy source on the following pages.

You Are In Control

By regularly measuring and analyzing the causes of your vibrancy or depletion, you can take 100% responsibility for your own energy. The good news is YOU are in control of the level of energy you are currently experiencing. **Event + Energy response = Outcome.** No matter what shows up in life, you have a choice in how you energetically respond. Be it your boss's attitude, the poor economy, irritable bickering children, the flu, the weather—whatever. When an "Event" appears in your life, it has already happened. You can't change it. The only way you can influence the next Outcome is by the way you think, the images you visualize and the actions you take, which all boil down to Energy

Responses. The responses you choose will either raise your energy or diminish it and will either get you closer or further away from the Outcome you want. Bringing awareness to these choices is a game-changer.

The more you take responsibility for the energy you bring to the world, the more empowered and productive you'll become.

High Performance Habits

The High Performing Woman is joyful, confident and fully engaged in her career, relationships and health and has strategies in place for consistently living from her best self. According to extensive global research done by *The High Performance Institute*, there are 6 habits that help you achieve consistent, long-term success above standard norms. They also correspond to areas on the Energy Engagement Wheel. The six high performance habits are:

1) seeking **clarity** (MindEnergy)
2) generating **energy** (the entire energy engagement wheel)
3) raising **necessity** (MindEnergy)
4) increasing **productivity** (the entire energy engagement wheel)
5) developing **influence** (**ConnectionEnergy**) and,
6) demonstrating **courage** (MindEnergy).

TAKE 100% RESPONSIBILITY FOR YOUR ENERGY LEVELS. GREATER ENERGY AWARENESS WILL EMPOWER YOU.

CHAPTER 3

INPUTENERGY

The higher your energy level, the more efficient your body, the better you feel and the more you will use your talent to produce outstanding results."

—Tony Robbins

INPUTENERGY

THE FIRST SLICE of pie on the Energy Engagement Wheel is for InputEnergy—the energy we get from the quality and quantity of the air, food, water, sleep and supplements we take into our bodies.

This is really the foundation of our energy. If you haven't got this right, no amount of energy from other areas will make up for it. Nothing can spring a leak in your energy pot faster than dinner at the golden arches of "McD's" and getting to bed at 3.

Studies have shown that people need:

- on average, 7-9 hours of sleep per night (sleeping less than 6 is the biggest predictor of on-the-job burnout)

- clean fresh[1] air

- 4% of their body weight in kilograms consumed in litres of purified[2] water per day (60kg (132lb) = 2.4 litres of water). 75% of Americans are chronically dehydrated.

- a diet rich in green, alkaline foods (sorry, green *m&m's* don't count!)

- high quality supplements (Omega3, Vitamin D, Magnesium & Selenium) and,

- prebiotics, multi-strain probiotics and digestive enzymes (no, I am afraid a "good" diet is just not enough in our soil depleted and processed food culture)

Did you know about 90% of your happy hormone serotonin is made in your gut? (Unhappy gut = unhappy you) Of course, always check with your doctor before starting any new supplements.

WHAT IS CHARACTERISTIC OF A FAVORABLE INPUTENERGY DIAGNOSIS?

A 10/10 might look like a strong immune system, feeling well-rested, having clear skin and eyes, being hydrated with purified[2] water, thriving on an alkaline diet with quality supplements and breathing in fresh[1], clean air.

Do you know that feeling you get when you have exercised, had a great night's sleep and a healthy meal? Why not put automatic habits in place to recreate that every day? The Average American is getting 6.5 hours of sleep, does not take regular exercise, is chronically dehydrated and has a diet high in processed foods, sugar and saturated fats. But this is *not* the High Performing Woman!

---

1   fresh air means air free from exhaust fumes, fumes from household cleaning supplies and chemical laden household items, dust mites, mold and mildew.

2   purified water means water free from pesticides, chemicals, pharmaceuticals, Chlorine and Fluoride which has not been stored in plastic.

MAXIMISE YOUR INPUTENERGY

Even the healthiest set of beliefs can't make up for sleep exhaustion, a damaged microbiome and dehydration.

Look for #InputEnergy ideas amongst the 52 Take Action Tips.

WHAT IS ONE NEW, HEALTHY INPUTENERGY ACTION YOU COULD TAKE TODAY?

———————————————

"Energy is more valuable than intelligence."

— Robin Sharma

CHAPTER 4

MindEnergy

"The energy of the mind is the essence of life."

— Aristotle

MindEnergy

THE SECOND SLICE of pie on the Energy Engagement Wheel is for MindEnergy—the energy generated by the thoughts you think, the images you visualise, the things that you seek and the way that you organize yourself.

Thinking negative thoughts, visualising negative outcomes, living inauthentically by not following your purpose and passions and being disorganised are all things that can drain your MindEnergy and lead to overwhelm and burnout.

Did you know that 51% of the U.S. workforce is not engaged? (2017 Gallup survey). This is a major MindEnergy leak and is costing organisations $450 to $550 billion annually (The Engagement Institute).

"When you are enthusiastic about what you do, you feel this positive energy. It's very simple."

— Paulo Coelho

Did you also know that most people have about 50,000 thoughts per day? And, that 70-80% are negative? The National Science Foundation says 95% are habitual. So, that is a whole lot of worrying, critical, self-sabotaging nonsense!

Our thoughts create our feelings and our feelings create our experience of life. So, choose them wisely!

> *"Just as your car runs more smoothly and requires less energy to go faster and farther when the wheels are in perfect alignment, you perform better when your thoughts, feelings, emotions, goals, and values are in balance."*

— Brian Tracy

WHAT IS CHARACTERISTIC OF A FAVORABLE MINDENERGY DIAGNOSIS?

A 10/10 might look like an attitude of positivity and gratitude; organized and productive to the point of automaticity; clarity regarding your purpose and passions and how to show up as your best self; courage; having a vision; clear on your values and living them congruently; confidence and high self-esteem.

MAXIMISE YOUR MINDENERGY

You only have control over 3 things in life. The thoughts you think, the images you visualize and the actions you take (there might not always be plentiful options, but you do always have an energetic choice about your attitude).

Look for #MindEnergy ideas amongst the 52 Take Action Tips.

WHAT IS ONE NEW, HEALTHY MINDENERGY ACTION YOU COULD TAKE TODAY?

"Passion is energy. Feel the power that comes from focusing on what excites you."

— Oprah Winfrey

CHAPTER 5

CONNECTIONENERGY

"It's so important to realize that every time you get upset, it drains your emotional energy. Losing your cool makes you tired. Getting angry a lot messes with your health."

— Joyce Meyer

CONNECTIONENERGY

THE THIRD SLICE of pie on the Energy Engagement Wheel is for ConnectionEnergy—the energy generated by how you communicate and interact with others.

This is where self-awareness plays a big part. Be responsible and intentional about the energy that you create and bring to others, as it is likely to be reflected in the energy they give back to you. *People remember your energy, not what you say.*

Positivity is contagious. As is complaining and gossiping. Try a negativity detox for a week. No blaming, complaining or gossiping for an entire week. This can be quite an eye-opener for some.

Introversion and Extroversion also play a big part in connection energy. Understanding and being aware of the nature and amount of connection/interaction that is optimal for you, as well as for the people in your circle of influence, is so important. Introverts will find too much social interaction draining whereas Extroverts will find being left on their own too much to be energy-draining.

Think about the quality of your key relationships. Take a moment to jot down the 5 people you spend the most time with. It could be work colleagues, friends, family members, etc.

Would you put a plus or minus next to them based on whether they generally bring you up or down?

For the ones with minuses, what new thinking or behaviours associated with those people could you choose to generate more connection energy? Sometimes, to preserve your ConnectionEnergy, you may even have to limit your exposure to certain individuals.

You can't change other people, but you can always change the language, tone and actions you use with them to get more positive reactions.

WHAT IS CHARACTERISTIC OF A FAVORABLE CONNECTIONENERGY DIAGNOSIS?

A 10/10 might look like positive, energizing relationships with the people in your circle of influence; giving and receiving good customer service; having intimacy and passion with your significant other; possessing strong personal leadership; being authentic; being present; having high EQ; and being adept at minimizing and managing conflict.

MAXIMISE YOUR CONNECTIONENERGY

So, do the ways you choose to interact and connect with others categorize you as an energy vampire or an energy angel?

Look for #ConnectionEnergy ideas amongst the 52 Take Action Tips.

WHAT IS ONE NEW, HEALTHY CONNECTIONENERGY ACTION YOU COULD TAKE TODAY?

"The most important single ingredient in the formula of success is the knack of getting along with people."

— Theodore Roosevelt

CHAPTER 6

PAUSEENERGY

"It is a very good plan every now and then to go away and have a little relaxation... when you come back to the work your judgment will be surer, since to remain constantly at work will cause you to lose the power of judgment."

— Leonardo Da Vinci

PAUSEENERGY

THE FOURTH SLICE of pie on the Energy Engagement Wheel is for PauseEnergy—the energy generated when you unplug, tune in, slow down, get still and connect to yourself and your spiritual source.

According to research at the University of Illinois at Urbana-Champaign, the brain gradually stops registering a sight, sound or feeling if that stimulus remains constant over time. You lose your focus, and your performance on the task declines.

Have you ever noticed that you have some of your best ideas when you PAUSE and allow time to be lost in thought? Like when you are in the shower or driving in the car or walking in nature?

Mindfulness, regular breaks of deep abdominal breathing, staring at art and nature and meditation all fall into this category.

You'll find taking deliberate 10-minute breaks in your day will allow the energy and ideas that come from getting still to seep in and allow the things that don't matter to fade away.

WHAT IS CHARACTERISTIC OF A FAVORABLE PAUSEENERGY DIAGNOSIS?

A 10/10 might look like regularly connecting with your source of spirituality; getting still and quite; being mindful; meditating; detoxifying from digital devices; spending time on hobbies; and moments of wonder with the arts and nature.

MAXIMISE YOUR PAUSEENERGY

Are you a roadrunner adrenaline junkie or do you take time out to go for a stroll and to reflect and recharge?

Look for #PauseEnergy ideas amongst the 52 Take Action Tips.

WHAT IS ONE NEW, HEALTHY PAUSEENERGY ACTION YOU COULD TAKE TODAY?

_____

"Love the moment and the energy of that moment will spread beyond all boundaries."

— Corita Kent

CHAPTER 7

MOVEENERGY

"Your body language shapes who you are."

— Prof. Amy Cuddy

MOVEENERGY

THE FIFTH SLICE of pie on the Energy Engagement Wheel is for MoveEnergy—the energy generated from the moves and shapes we give our bodies, from body language to exercise.

Are you hunched over your iPhone or computer all day or do you practice your Professor Amy Cuddy "power pose" (see her TED Talk) and great posture and pursue an active lifestyle?

"Smile—even if you don't feel like it. Your body language helps determine your state of mind."

— Gitte Falkenberg

Sitting is the new smoking. Did you know, as soon as you sit, electrical activity in your legs shuts off, enzymes that break down fat drop by 90%, and after two hours of sitting, your good cholesterol drops?

Exercise isn't just a vanity project—it's about much more than just looking good or losing weight. It lifts our mood, helps us focus, gives us *energy* and leads to innovative and creative ideas. And…the latest neuroscience research has demonstrated that increased levels of physical exercise can result in improved memory by enhancing both the birth rate and the survival of new hippocampal brain cells.

Exercise encourages the long-term growth of hippocampal cells by immediately increasing levels of a key growth factor in the hippocampus called Brain Derived Neurotrophic Factor (BDNF). So, the more regularly you exercise throughout your life, the more healthy, young hippocampal cells you build up, which lower your chances of suffering from cognitive decline and dementia as you age.

WHAT IS CHARACTERISTIC OF A FAVORABLE MoveEnergy Diagnosis?

A 10/10 might look like good posture, confident body language, regular movement and exercise, and smiles!

Maximise your MoveEnergy

The fastest way to change your energy is to change your physiology.
Look for #MoveEnergy ideas amongst the 52 Take Action Tips.

What is one new, healthy MoveEnergy action you could take today?

_____

"Our bodies have evolved to move, yet we now use the energy in oil instead of our muscles to do our work."

— David Suzuki

CHAPTER 8

SPACEENERGY

SPACEENERGY

THE SIXTH AND final slice of pie on the Energy Engagement Wheel is for SpaceEnergy—the energy you generate from the material objects and environments you choose to surround yourself with.

This can be office, home and holiday environments as well as the material possessions in these environments.

> *"The most important thing to understand is that feng shui is really about the energy that's surrounding you in your personal space."*
>
> — Lillian Too

> *It can also be colors, smells and sounds...* *"With color one obtains an energy that seems to stem from witchcraft."*
>
> — Henri Matisse

Even the garments and personal care products you put on your body space can generate energy or take it away.

"My style motto is pretty classic; you give off a positive energy when you wear what you are comfortable in."

— Petra Collins

Is your space crushed under clutter and chaos? Closets full but nothing to wear?

Or do you have space for your creativity to flourish and room to let in the new and good?

Cluttered space is like a physical representation of a big undone to-do list. Having things in your space that irritate you and that you tolerate will energetically chip away at you. Are there things in your space that provoke a negative thought or a big sigh throughout your day? These can be things directly on your body space, like a poor fitting bra or shoes that pinch. Or, it could be a chip in your wind screen and a full email inbox.

When you free yourself from the mental burden of SPACE drains, you'll be AMAZED at how quickly the things you do want in life arrive.

"Clutter clearing is modern day alchemy."

— Denise Linn

WHAT IS CHARACTERISTIC OF A FAVORABLE SPACEENERGY DIAGNOSIS?

A 10/10 might look like garments and shoes that fit well and feel good, ergonomic workspace, a comfortable bed/home, being surrounded by objects/views that inspire (like a vision board) and desired scents and sounds.

MAXIMISE YOUR SPACEENERGY

Are you energised by your surroundings and is your physical space and surroundings representative of the person you are becoming?

"When you surround yourself with possessions that spark joy, you'll create a home and life you love."

— Marie Kondo

Look for #SpaceEnergy ideas amongst the 52 Take Action Tips.

WHAT IS ONE NEW, HEALTHY SPACEENERGY ACTION YOU COULD TAKE TODAY?

_____

"Closing the closet doors makes the mess go away."

— said no Feng Shui consultant ever

CHAPTER 9

YOUR ENERGY DIAGNOSIS

"The secret to change is to focus all of your energy, not on fighting the old, but on building the new."

— Socrates

SO, WHAT IS YOUR DIAGNOSIS?

TAKE OUT THAT piece of paper and copy down the Energy Engagement Wheel from Chapter 2. Now spend some time analyzing where your energy comes from and where it goes. Plot your scores on the wheel.

WHERE IS YOUR BIGGEST ENERGY LEAK?

What is, currently, the greatest source of your depletion? What is blocking your full engagement? What sort of negative habits are blocking, contaminating, distorting, wasting, diminishing and depleting your stored energy?

Clutter? -SPACE

Negative thinking? -MIND

Poor body language? -MOVE

Poor diet? -INPUTS

No down time? -PAUSE

Stressful relationship(s)? -CONNECTION

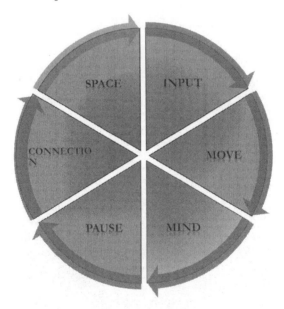

WHAT IS YOUR PREFERRED SOURCE OF CREATING ENERGY AND VIBRANCY?

Do you seek SpaceEnergy by:
Going to your own special zen place,
Having a big clear out,
Or having a mass deletion and unsubscribing purge on your computer?

Do you seek MindEnergy by:
Thinking positive thoughts,
Reading your affirmations and focusing on your vision of success,
Or thinking of things that you are grateful for?

Do you create PauseEnergy by:
Taking a stroll through nature,
Meditating,
Or practicing mindfulness?

Do you seek ConnectionEnergy by:
Looking for a hug,
Or calling an energy angel friend to meet for a coffee?

Do you use InputEnergy as a pick-me-up by:
Eating a healthy meal,
Getting a good night's rest,
Or simply drinking a glass of water?

Do you create MoveEnergy by:
Going for a run,
Straightening up your posture,
Or looking up with a smile?

SIMPLY BRINGING AWARENESS TO WHERE YOUR ENERGY COMES FROM AND WHERE IT GOES WILL KICKSTART THE PROCESS OF CHANGE.

CHAPTER 10

YOUR PERSONAL ENERGY PLAN

"Start by doing what's necessary; then do what's possible; and suddenly you are doing the impossible."

— St. Francis of Assisi

NOW IT'S TIME TO WRITE YOUR ENERGY PRESCRIPTION!

IT'S ALL WELL and good knowing where your energy goes, but what matters is what you do about it.

Instead of saying

"I have no time for the gym, so my MOVE energy is low"

or

"My boss annoys me, and my husband doesn't appreciate me, and my kids are so demanding, so my CONNECTION energy is low," take responsibility for your outcomes—your thoughts, visualisations and behaviors.

The definition of insanity is doing the same thing over and expecting a different result.

START BY INTRODUCING SMALL NEW ENERGY HABITS

Use the *Take Action Tips* and the High Performance Habits now to start creating some easy energy rituals to plug up the leaks and add more as your energy grows.

WORK TOWARDS AUTOMATICITY

"There isn't anything that isn't made easier through constant familiarity and training. Through training we can change; we can transform ourselves."

— Dalai Lama

In other words, create rituals that become easy and automatic, like brushing your teeth. The more you can automatize, the more energy you can conserve for the important things in life.

COMMIT TO TAKING ONE NEW ENERGY ACTION PER WEEK.

―――――――――――――

Take Action Tip 1

Win Your Morning

"It's not the will to win, but the will to prepare to win that makes the difference."

— Paul Bryant

I HAVE BEEN writing weekly tips *for greater positivity, productivity and purpose in your personal and professional life* for several years now and I often get asked: "What is your very top tip?" That is a bit like asking, "How long is a piece of string?" It depends. The top tip is one that resonates with you and moves you to *take positive action*. That said, I do have a personal favourite (which actually encompasses several tips). So, drum roll please...

My top life hack and Take Action Tip is to win your morning. If you can win the morning (at least the first hour) you usually win the day. Winning your morning means recognising that *you* are the main one that creates the results in your life. Your thoughts, the pictures you visualise in your head and how you respond (your actions) to what shows up, create your experience of life. So, work out a morning routine that will set you up for a better experience. This will *not* include reaching for your device first thing to scroll through the convenient organising program of other people's agendas (email) or the addictive, FOMO-judgement platform (a.k.a. Facebook).

10 Tried and tested actions to *win your morning* are as follows:

- **Write down at least 3 new things you are grateful for.** Studies have shown that people who practice an attitude of gratitude have less stress and depression, more resilience and energy and improved sleep and immune systems.

- **Meditate.** For the same positive side effects and more.

- **Prioritise your one big task for the day.** Then make sure you *Eat that Frog* first thing.

- **Set your intentions for the day.** Look at what is on the day's agenda and decide how you want to show up and feel. What would make today great?

- **Decide who you can appreciate or reach out to that day.** And then plan to positively surprise them.

- **Repeat a positive affirmation.** Every cell in your body is eavesdropping on your thoughts.

- **Drink a glass of water.** We are chronically dehydrated.

- **Move your body.** Do some stretching, strength training, yoga, etc. Get it in early before you sit all day (the new smoking). Even a few minutes per day can make a difference.

- **Read** something that will make you healthier, wealthier or wiser. Just a passage or a few pages can inspire, entertain, educate and motivate.

- **Make your bed!** Accomplishing the first simple task of the day gives you momentum and much more. (See Admiral William H. McRaven's Commencement Address at U. of Texas in 2014.)

Work out a morning routine to create a life you don't want a vacation from. Like bathing, it's best done daily!

So, what are you going to do to get off to a winning start?

"It is well to be up before daybreak, for such habits contribute to health, wealth and wisdom."

— Aristotle

ASK YOURSELF "WHAT IS ONE THING I CAN ADD TO MY MORNING RITUAL THAT WILL HELP ME WIN MY DAY?"

———————————

#Clarity #Productivity #PauseEnergy #MoveEnergy #MindEnergy #InputEnergy

Take Action Tip 2

Stop Playing It Safe

"Who will I be if I stay?"

—Wonder Woman

HAVE YOU SEEN the latest Wonder Woman movie with Gal Gadot? Loved it! To me it was a film about how we are defined by our choices. There is good and bad, brave and weak in all of us. Who we are and become is simply down to our choices.

There were lots of great quotes throughout the film, but the one that stuck in my mind was, "Who will I be if I stay?" Diana says this to her mother, Queen Hippolyta, who is trying to convince her to stay safe on the Amazonian island of Themyscira instead of going to make a difference in the mortal world at war.

Although I do not hail from Themyscira, this concept resonates with me and is a question that I have often asked myself. Who will I be if I stay in this job, this relationship, in this place of stuck-ness? Will I really be safe if I play it safe?

If your choices lately have been to stay where you are (physically, mentally, spiritually), instead of growing and thriving, **Today's Take Action Tip is to ask yourself, "Who will I be if I stay?"**

Who will you be:

- if you stay in your current job?

- if you stay in your current relationship?
- if you stay communicating the way you do?
- if you keep playing it safe?
- if you don't make that change?

Successful change often requires clarity on both your "away from" motivation (what you *don't* want—the pain you are trying to avoid) **as well your "toward" motivation** (what you *do* want).

So, who will *you* be if you "stay"?

> "Sometimes you make choices in life and sometimes choices make you."
>
> — Gayle Forman, If I Stay

ASK YOURSELF, "WHO WILL I BE IF I REFUSE TO MAKE SOME CHANGES?"

#Clarity #Courage #Necessity #MindEnergy

TAKE ACTION TIP 3

IMPROVE YOUR DIET

"Let food be thy medicine and medicine be thy food."

— Hippocrates

WE ALL KNOW that eating a healthy diet is good for us and "you are what you eat," so how come so many of us are willing to be "Fast," "Cheap," "Easy" and "Fake"? As a holistic executive coach, I have seen that a good diet is one of the biggest catalysts for personal and professional success. Yet many people that come to me for coaching are regularly consuming a combination of: takeaways at their desks, big (boozy) meals with clients, multiple daily coffees, mid-afternoon sweet "treats" and airline food. And, surprise, surprise, they have brain fog and are too low in energy to make the changes they want in life.

So, **Today's Take Action Tip is to improve your diet. Give yourself food for thought (literally).**

To follow are my top 3 tips to aid your peak performance via your diet:

1) **Eat less sugar** – We've known for ages that sugar helps pack on the pounds and rots your teeth. But it has now been shown to stir up inflammation that is a leading cause of heart disease, it feeds cancer cells, it weakens your immune system, it stresses

your pancreas (increasing your risk of Type 2 diabetes), and every single teaspoon of sugar decreases your body's supply of B vitamins, and B vitamins are crucial for mental performance (especially B12). Actions: Above all, eliminate anything with High Fructose Corn Syrup in it. Drink water instead of soda or sports drinks (pink Lucozade =17.5 tsp sugar vs the NHS daily recommendation of 7.5 tsp per day). Check out easy "food swaps" to cut down on sugar. See link below.

2) **Use natural antibiotics** – Feel like you are coming down with a cold or that your immune system is struggling? Actions: Up your garlic, goldenseal, echinacea, ginger and Manuka honey. Save prescription antibiotics for life-threatening emergencies.

3) **Eat "real" food** – Actions: Eat food as it is found in nature, i.e., organic where possible, mostly plant, non-GMO and not in a bag, box or tin can. Check out the 2016 Food Revolution Summit for inspiration. Link below.

So, what are you going to consume (or not) today for greater clarity and energy?

"I really regret eating healthily today."

—said no-one EVER

Useful links:

Easy food swaps to reduce sugar:
http://www.dailymail.co.uk/femail/food/article-3178341/What-Coca-Cola-REALLY-does-body-just-hour.html

The Food Revolution Network:
https://foodrevolution.org/

ASK YOURSELF, "WHAT IS ONE THING I CAN DO TO IMPROVE MY DIET TODAY?"

#Clarity #Energy #InputEnergy

TAKE ACTION TIP 4

GIVE YOURSELF
SOME ADVICE

"The only thing to do with good advice is to pass it on."

— Oscar Wilde

WE'VE ALL MADE mistakes in our careers at some point and, looking back with 20/20 hindsight, we can see clearly now a much less circuitous route from A to B than the path we followed. So, **Today's Take Action Tip is to ask yourself: "What career/business advice would I give my younger self?"**

Taking Oscar Wilde's advice, I am passing on the good advice that friends, colleagues and clients shared with me at one of my book launches. In response to the question, "What career/business advice would you give to your younger self?" here are a few of the pearls of wisdom that I gleaned:

- **Listen to your gut** and know it will all work out well.

- **Don't try to do it all at once.** Despite seeing so many areas where you can make a difference…plan and be on top of your game and improve steadily.

- **Embrace technology faster!**

- **Follow your passions**—not what your parents want you to do.

- **Spend time networking and raising your profile.** Don't assume your boss is doing it for you.

- **Learn how to say NO gracefully!**

- **Get a sponsor and a mentor** and understand their different roles in your career.

- **Don't avoid public speaking** because you hate it. Sooner or later you will have to do it, so practice, practice, practice!

- **Believe in yourself!**

- **Be aware of your posture** and grow your executive presence.

And of course, my favourite:

- **Get a coach!**

So what advice would YOU give to your younger self? And what advice would you still give yourself now? Then why not take it?

"No one can give you better advice than yourself."

— Marcus Tullius Cicero

ASK YOURSELF, "WHAT IS ONE PIECE OF ADVICE I WOULD GIVE TO MY YOUNGER SELF? AND AM I FOLLOWING IT?"

#Clarity #Energy #Influence #Productivity #MindEnergy
#ConnectionEnergy #MoveEnergy

TAKE ACTION TIP 5

SAY "YES, AND..."

BUILDING YOUR "No" repertoire helps you gracefully decline requests for your time and attention. There are also times when "Yes" is effective too. **Today's Take Action Tip is to say, "Yes, and…" more often!**

Confused? Just to clarify, I am *not* suggesting that you answer "yes" to more requests of your time and attention. What I *am* saying is that using a "Yes, and…" response structure is another way for saying "no" gracefully or for disagreeing tactfully.

The power of starting with a "yes" shows the other person that they have been heard and that you haven't merely been waiting for your turn to speak. It can also be more motivating. **Beginning your responses with a "No," "However" or "But" blocks effective communication, collaboration and connection. It also prompts defensive reactions.**

Consider the following exchanges:

"I think my sales pitch went well today."
"But I think it could have gone better if you'd summarised with 3 key points at the end."
vs.
"Yes, and next time I think you will knock it out of the park with 3 key summary points."

"Did you like the roast chicken dinner with mashed potatoes I made you last night?"

"It was good. **However,** I would have preferred roast potatoes."
vs.
"**Yes! And** do you know what? I bet roast potatoes could go really well with it too."

"I think we should go on holiday to the states this year."
"**No**—I really don't want to go there. I'd rather go to Mexico this year."
vs.
"**Yes!** A holiday somewhere different would be great. **And** I think we could consider Mexico as well."

The way we choose to interact and communicate with others can add or detract from our energy and leadership presence.

So, what are you going to say, "Yes, and…" to today?

"The oldest, shortest words – 'yes' and 'no' – are those that require the most thought."

— Pythagoras

ASK YOURSELF, "HOW CAN I GRACIOUSLY DISAGREE OR PROVIDE FEEDBACK TODAY USING 'YES, AND…'?"

#Influence #Productivity #MindEnergy #ConnectionEnergy #MoveEnergy

TAKE ACTION TIP 6

BE INTERESTED

"You can make more friends in two months by becoming interested in other people than you can in two years by trying to get other people interested in you."

— Dale Carnegie

EVERYBODY BENEFITS FROM quality, energising connections. Personal relationships rule the world. No matter where you are on this planet, things simply get done via personal and professional networks. And positive relationships are also one of the few sources of sustainable, authentic happiness (Source - Martin Seligman, founder of the positive psychology movement).

So, to get you started in building a network of positive relationships, **Today's Take Action Tip is to be "interested"** (as well as interesting). Be genuinely interested in other people…and in a bizarre twist of quantum psychology, people will find you insanely interesting as a result.

To follow are some **suggestions on how to be authentically interested in others:**

- **Make Eye Contact.** Many people in today's busy world feel unseen and unappreciated. When you make eye contact and choose to be completely present with someone, it cultivates a level of trust and safety that allows them to open up to you.

- **Ask loads of questions about them.** People generally love talking about themselves, and asking a few well-chosen questions have the interesting psychological effect of making you seem more interesting. Ask what she's reading. What does she like and dislike, and why? What bothers him out there in the world? How would he fix it if he had a magic wand? Ask her about current events but be genuine—the questioning should not be a "tactic." Choose topics you are genuinely interested in—people can tell when you are faking interest—and remember to listen to their answers instead of thinking/talking about your own opinions.

- **Listen for how you can be helpful.** Even the biggest and most powerful people in the world have something they'd like help with. Listen with the intent of how you can help someone you've just met instead of selling yourself or trying to be interesting. Relationships are built over multiple instances of connection, and having a reason to follow up later adds another point of contact. If it turns out you can't be that helpful, the gesture alone will still stand out.

So, who are you going to take an interest in today? Where could a positive connection be mutually beneficial?

> *"You have to be interested. If you're not interested, you can't be interesting."*
>
> —Iris Apfel

ASK YOURSELF, "WHO AM I GOING TO LISTEN TO WITH ALL OF MY SENSES TODAY?"

#Influence #ConnectionEnergy

TAKE ACTION TIP 7

REDUCE ANONYMITY

*"I believe the biggest gift I can conceive of having from any-
one is to be seen by them, heard by them, to be understood
and touched by them."*

— Virginia Satir

THE NUMBER ONE common denominator in the human experience is that we all want to know we are seen and heard. As
social beings, which we all are, we need to feel connected with
others to thrive. Connection is essential for our overall wellbeing. It
opens the door to sharing our unique thoughts, talents and gifts. Most
people understand this intuitively with friends and family, yet often
neglect to connect with the people they work for, with or manage. This
is why 82% of employees say their organizations have an employee engagement problem according to the Psychometrics Engagement Study.

In Patrick Lencioni's book, *The Three Signs of a Miserable Job*, one
of the three tell-tale signs is "anonymity"; basically, not working with
anyone that knows and cares about you as a person outside of work.

So, **Today's Take Action Tip is to take the time to connect with
someone in your sphere of influence.** Whether that removes your own
anonymity or that of someone else, either way it will raise your connection energy.

Based on research by the Gallup Organisation, the top performing organisations with the highest productivity and performance had employees that answered "yes" to most of the following 12 questions:

1) Do I know what is expected of me at work?

2) Do I have the materials and equipment I need to do my job?

3) Do I have the opportunity to do what I do best every day?

4) In the past seven days, have I received recognition or praise for good work?

5) Does my supervisor, or someone at work, seem to care about me as a person?

6) Is there someone at work who encourages my development?

7) At work, do my opinions seem to count?

8) Does the mission/purpose of my company make me feel my job is important?

9) Are my co-workers committed to doing quality work?

10) Do I have a close friend at work?

11) In the last six months, has someone talked to me about my progress?

12) This last year, have I had opportunities to learn and grow?

Disengagement is not the only result of "anonymity." You will also not fare well in your appraisals and your promotion efforts will be hampered. Research shows that the greatest factor in getting promoted is your profile. How are you perceived and who knows you and is willing to sponsor you?

If you aren't answering yes to most of these questions above, what could you do to erase anonymity and increase connection in your life and/or organisation?

"There's nothing more daring than showing up, putting ourselves out there and letting ourselves be seen."

— Brené Brown

ASK YOURSELF, "HOW CAN I GET TO KNOW ONE PERSON BETTER TODAY AT WORK?"

#Courage #Clarity #Influence #Productivity #ConnectionEnergy #MindEnergy

Take Action Tip 8

Stop Self-Sabotage

"People don't resist change. They resist being changed!"

— Peter Senge

I'M NOT REALLY a gadget person, but, having been given a Fitbit for a recent birthday, I find it super simple to use and I love the challenge of trying to fit in at least 10,000 steps each day. Some days I easily fit in the steps without even trying, whilst other days I'm off the underground one stop earlier or parking at a distance to squeeze in my last few paces.

The power of public shaming has also resulted in positive changes…my children have been grabbing my wrist in public places to check on my paces and loudly admonishing me for my paltry progress—so I've literally had to *step up* my game.

What gets measured gets done.

In the midst, however, of these positive Fitbit-led fitness changes, I have a confession to make. I've caught myself on more than one occasion trying to "game" my device, scheming up ways to score a few extra steps to get to the illusive 10k per day, like taking loads of baby steps as I walk towards my front door at the end of the day or vigorously brushing my teeth using my Fitbit hand. I've even gone as far as perfecting a pace registering arm shake that looks a bit like I am frantically trying to fling a spider off my hand (not a good look).

But who am I trying to cheat? The thing about change is most of us dislike it and resist it, even when it is positive change and we want it and have initiated it.

So, **Today's Take Action Tip is to recognise the ways you stop yourself from making positive changes (aka, self-sabotage).** Do you:

- Get too busy – refuse to focus?

- Procrastinate?

- Focus on your fear…of success, failure, whatever, instead of what you want?

- Break commitments?

- Blame others?

- Think you are different – "The change doesn't apply/work for me." Other sabotage?

If so, stop it! Observe yourself objectively (what's really driving your behaviour?); don't be a perfectionist and give up on the desired change just because you veered slightly off course. If you won't make the change for yourself, think beyond yourself. How is your self-sabotage indirectly hurting others?

> *"It is not the strongest or the most intelligent who will survive but those who can best manage change."*
>
> — Charles Darwin

ASK YOURSELF, "WHAT IS ONE POSITIVE CHANGE I AM RESISTING MAKING?" AND MAKE IT!

#Clarity #Influence #Productivity #ConnectionEnergy #MindEnergy

TAKE ACTION TIP 9

TAKE OFF YOUR MASK

"Like Batman, all of us hide behind our masks and use them to help define ourselves for others. We all have secret identities of a sort, hidden behind our smiling social-networking profiles or our happy church faces. They're not lies, really. They're just not the whole truth, because we know that most of the people we encounter day-to-day couldn't handle the truth (or perhaps we couldn't handle giving it to them)."

— Paul Asay, God on the Streets of Gotham

M Y CHILDREN LOVE Halloween. What's not to love about eating sweets, dressing up and hiding behind masks? But for many of us, these sorts of behaviours aren't just for Halloween. **We all hide behind masks to be accepted, loved or even ignored.** Masks give us the cover necessary to gain acceptance by society. Being rejected by society can have serious implications, ranging from scorn to even exile or death in some places. But not everything is life or death. **Are you "managing perceptions" or an "approval addict"?** We can often feel an exhausting need to present an "ideal" image to the world and end up wearing masks that hide our true colours even when we don't really need to.

What masks do you wear? Serious corporate person? Eccentric? Ice maiden? Vamp? Clown? Intellectual? Concerned friend? Miss calm and collected? Miss organised? Lady? Joker? Victim? Bureaucrat? Drama queen?

When do you wear these masks? And what do you gain...or lose... by wearing them? Is the scariest place for you the place without your masks? Recognising when you put on certain masks will allow you to recognise the nature of your fears, which is the first step to overcoming them.

Today's Take Action Tip is to take off a mask. Authenticity is energising. Get better at being who you are. It is exhausting to consistently be someone you aren't. Not only will it boost your confidence and energy, it will also attract the right resources, opportunities and people to you.

> *"She had blue skin,*
> *And so did he.*
> *He kept it hid*
> *And so did she.*
> *They searched for blue*
> *Their whole life through,*
> *Then passed right by-*
> *And never knew."*

> — Shel Silverstein, *Everything on It*

> *"Wearing a mask wears you out. Faking it is fatiguing. The most exhausting activity is pretending to be what you know you aren't."*

> — Rick Warren

ASK YOURSELF, "HOW CAN I SHOW UP MORE AUTHENTICALLY TODAY?"

#Courage #Influence #Energy #ConnectionEnergy #MindEnergy

TAKE ACTION TIP 10

BE HUMBLE

"True humility is not thinking less of yourself; it is thinking of yourself less."

— C.S. Lewis

IN MY EXPERIENCE, "I"-centred individuals usually crowd out everybody else to make room for their egos. There is no room for followers, and you can't be a leader without having at least one follower. Which is why in *"Good to Great"* by Jim Collins, genuine personal humility is one of the characteristics commonly found in truly great leaders.

Besides making you a more relatable leader, having humility reduces stress and worry and can make you a better parent and good role model.

So, **Today's Take Action Tip is to practice humility:**

- **Try using 'we'** when taking credit – not just when explaining less than stellar outcomes.

- **Stop trying to prove yourself to others**. Allowing some weakness to be seen creates vulnerability and sharing your vulnerability shows your strength.

- **Disconnect your sense of value and worth from the outcome.** You are valuable and worthy regardless of external variables.

- **Work to be accepting of your present situation** while striving for more without complaining.
- **Accept contradictions and correction with grace.** Assume positive intent from all feedback.
- **Speak less about yourself and show more interest in others** (which will, of course, immediately make you more interesting).

Don't mistake insecurity and inadequacy for humility. Humility has nothing to do with those qualities just as arrogance has nothing to do with greatness.

> *"What the world needs is more geniuses with humility, there are so few of us left."*

— Oscar Levant

ASK YOURSELF, "HOW CAN I SERVE OTHERS TODAY?"

#Courage #Influence #ConnectionEnergy #MindEnergy

TAKE ACTION TIP 11

DISPLAY WISDOM

"Knowledge is knowing what to say. Wisdom is knowing when to say it."

— Unknown

WHEN STRESSFUL EVENTS happen, how we interpret them often matters even more than the event itself. Wisdom whispers, *"Wait a little while, until the emotions settle down, before you do or say something. Then check to see if you really believe it's the right thing to do."* Emotions urge us to haste, telling us, *"You must do something and do it right now."* Our natural tendency is to focus on what our emotion is saying and when we focus on it, we can magnify it in ways that aren't always helpful. **One of the biggest challenges we face when making decisions is overestimating the importance of our immediate emotions.**

Stephen Hall, who wrote *Wisdom: from Philosophy to Neuroscience*, argues that there's an important distinction between being smart and being wise. **True wisdom is characterized by the ability to manage your emotions, even when things aren't going your way.** Which means being able to resist the impulse to do something, anything, just for the sake of taking action. And critically, it requires the ability to step back and reframe complex situations. Easier said than done!

If you find it difficult to refrain from saying too much in an emotional moment, **Today's Take Action Tip is to set the intent to reframe the next situation when you're drowning in emotion.**

- Ask yourself: *"How will I feel about this event 10 hours, 10 days, and 10 years from now?"*
- Or as the comedian Craig Ferguson says:
- *"Does this need to be said?"*
- *"Does this need to be said by me?"*
- *"Does this need to be said by me now?"*

Usually, this line of questioning leads to wiser decisions. How you feel and what you want to say today will not be how you feel tomorrow. And it will certainly not be how you feel in 10 years.

So, which questions might be helpful to ask yourself the next time a bit of wisdom is called for?

> *"Speak when you are angry, and you will make the best speech you'll ever regret."*
>
> — Lawrence J. Peter

ASK YOURSELF, "IN WHICH SITUATIONS WILL I DISPLAY WISDOM TODAY?"

#Clarity #Influence #ConnectionEnergy #MindEnergy

TAKE ACTION TIP 12

TIMING IS EVERYTHING

"The right thing at a wrong time is a wrong thing."

— Joshua Harris

TIMING, AS THE saying goes, is everything.
I recently listened to some of Ron Friedman's Peak Performance Summit and it struck me that a lot of **what makes us successful comes down to timing**.

"Success is simple. Do what's right, the right way at the right time."

— Arnold H. Glasow.

Or, *not* so simple, as the case may be. Does doing what's right in the right way come easier to you than doing it at the right time?

If so, **Today's Take Action Tip is to consider your timing.**

To follow are some useful timing tips I have come across:

Best time to speak: To know, ask yourself: Does this need to be said? Does this need to be said by me? And does this need to be said by me now?

Best time to make a request: According to research by Michael Breus, to get a favourable response, make your "big requests" on Fridays, after lunch. It's when your boss or client will likely be most amenable to your request.

Best time to multi-task: According to Christine Carter, combining a physical activity (like doing the dishes) with a mental activity (like idea generation) can be a very effective use of your time. It's the blending of two physical tasks or two mental tasks that you should avoid.

Best time to listen: When emotions are high, or you are in conflict, try asking one more question and really listen before leaping in to talk. Jump to action and advice just a little bit slower.

So, what can you do to tweak your timing today?

As for the best **time to take action?** – Tuesday is, statistically, the most productive day of the week.

> *"Right time, right place, right people equals success. Wrong time, wrong place, wrong people equals most of the real human history."*

— Idries Shah

ASK YOURSELF, "HOW ARE YOU GOING TO BE STRATEGIC IN YOUR TIMINGS TODAY?"

#Clarity #Influence #Productivity #ConnectionEnergy #MindEnergy

TAKE ACTION TIP 13

HAVE SOME
FRIENDS - WITH
BENEFITS

"Without friends, no one would want to live, even if he had all other goods."

— Aristotle

IN SPITE OF current received wisdom that happiness is an inside job, **our happiness actually depends on other people.** Research shows that having friends (even *more* so than close relationships with family) is key to our happiness *and* health. Study after study shows that good social relationships are the strongest, most consistent predictor there is of a happy life. And there are also health benefits to having more friends. A clinical review (link below) involving more than 300,000 individuals found that people with strong friendships have a 50 percent better chance of survival, regardless of age, sex, health status and cause of death, than those with weaker ties. In fact, according to research, the health risk of **having few friends is similar to smoking 15 cigarettes a day,** and more dangerous than being obese or not exercising in terms of decreasing your lifespan.

Yet social interaction is declining. The average American eats about half of their meals alone now and only spends around half an hour a day on "real" world social communication with friends (doing the thumb scroll through Facebook on your smartphone doesn't count) compared to three hours per day watching TV.

So, if you want to live a longer and happier life (and enjoy your job more), **Today's Take Action Tip is to focus on your friendships.** To follow are some tips to grow and deepen your friendships:

1) **Be intentional about creating friendships at work** – Most people will spend more time with their work colleagues than their nearest and dearest. So why not forge some good friendships to reap the health and happiness benefits? One plus of Patrick Lencioni's *Three signs of a Miserable Job* was "Anonymity" - i.e., not working with at least one person who knows and cares about you as an individual. Having a friend at work is one of the 3 main requisites of a happy job and a Gallup survey showed that the highest performing companies have a greater than average number of employees with a close friend at work.

2) **Never eat alone** – No more desk dining! Make lunchtime, connection time. If you don't create friendships, you will at least create an amazing network. Check out Keith Ferrazi's *Never Eat Alone and Other Secrets to Success, One Relationship at a Time.*

3) **Nurture your most important friendships** – Support. Encourage. Help. Be vulnerable and real so that your friends can be too.

> *"A friend is someone who gives you total freedom to be yourself."*
>
> — Jim Morrison

So, what are you going to do to form great friendships?

"I value the friend who for me finds time on his calendar, but I cherish the friend who for me does not consult his calendar."

— Robert Brault

Ask Yourself, "Who Can I Eat Lunch With Today?"

#Clarity #Courage #Influence #ConnectionEnergy

TAKE ACTION TIP 14

BE STRATEGIC WITH YOUR CAREER

"You can have everything you want in life if you will just help enough other people get what they want."

— Zig Ziglar

EVERYONE LOVES A nice slice of pie. (Mine is gluten-free Pumpkin pie—which I do recognize is an acquired taste!) Portion control is of course important. Too big of a slice, too often doesn't lead to a good outcome. The same goes for your Career P.I.E. **slices;** **P**erformance, **I**mage and **E**xposure. These are the main components of a successful career…but most people get the size of their P.I.E. slices wrong.

According to Harvey Coleman in his book *Empowering Yourself, The Organizational Game Revealed*, most people focus the majority of their time on the *Performance* slice of their career. This means that they spend the bulk of their time head down, focussing simply on doing a good job. Sadly, that only counts for 10% of your success. *Image* counts for approximately 30% and *Exposure* counts for a whopping 60%.

So, **Today's Take Action Tip is to work on the size of your P.I.E. slices!**

Where do you need portion control with your P.I.E. slices?

1) **Performance:** This is about how well you do your job day-to-day and the quality of the results you deliver. Are you all about the project and the associated tasks?

2) **Image:** This is how other people perceive you. Your personal brand. Do you have confidence and gravitas? Do you look the part? Do you have a positive attitude and lead with solutions to issues, or are you always complaining and blocking change?

3) **Exposure:** Who knows you, what you do and is willing to sponsor you? Does your boss know all the good things you are up to? Does her boss know too? Do you invest in growing your network both inside and outside of your organisation?

If you want some tongue-in-cheek suggestions for raising your profile, increasing your confidence and managing perceptions, go to the link below!

So which P.I.E. slice will you work on today?

> *"We must have a pie. Stress cannot exist in the presence of a pie."*

> — David Mamet

https://www.linkedin.com/pulse/51-ways-eradicate-your-executive-presence-susan-treadgold?trk=mp-author-card

ASK YOURSELF, "AM I CLEAR WHO MY MENTORS AND SPONSORS ARE AND WHO I CAN COUNT ON IN MY NETWORK?"

#Clarity #Influence #ConnectionEnergy #MindEnergy

Take Action Tip 15

Negotiate

"Let us never negotiate out of fear. But let us never fear to negotiate."

— John F. Kennedy

A LMOST EVERY SORT of human interaction or communication involves negotiation, to a certain degree. Be it a new job offer, a big client deal or bedtime for your little one (children, by the way, are master negotiators). We even negotiate with ourselves. "Hmmm. Should I choose the blue one...or the red one?" Whatever the decision or task, **the ability to negotiate well is important for achieving successful outcomes.** When faced with a negotiation, are you like a dog with a bone? Do you "show your cards too early" or do you cave too easily? If so, and if you have a better outcome in mind, then **Today's Take Action Tip is to brush up on your negotiation skills.** To follow are some tips to bear in mind when negotiating:

1) **Know what your want is** – What, specifically, do you want to get out of the interaction? Have options. Know your **MFP** (most favoured position), your **FBP** (fall-back position - the worst outcome you'd accept) and your **BATNA** (best alternative to a negotiated agreement - what is plan B if you simply can't agree?).

2) **Know the other side** – Do your homework. Estimate what *they* want. Put yourself in their shoes. What do you think their "must haves" and "nice to haves" are? Look for overlap where you both can win.

3) **Hone your communication. Remain calm** – Smile and refrain from raising your voice. **Listen** – it helps build rapport. If you only focus on what *you* have to say, you may miss valuable information. **Start by agreeing** on something small first and build momentum from there. Save the most contentious points for later. **Pause.** Silence can be very effective resistance.

And…if you are looking for a new job, a top question to achieve a higher offer is, "If you can get me X, I'll accept the offer right away." It shows you're confident, want the job and it saves time on back and forth negotiation.

So, what are you going to negotiate for today?

> *"In business, you don't get what you deserve, you get what you negotiate."*

— Chester Karass

ASK YOURSELF, "AM I CLEAR WHO MY MENTORS AND SPONSORS ARE AND WHO I CAN COUNT ON IN MY NETWORK?"

#Clarity #Influence #Courage #ConnectionEnergy #MindEnergy

TAKE ACTION TIP 16

VALUE THE INTROVERTS IN YOUR LIFE

"Solitude matters, and for some people, it's the air they breathe."

— Susan Cain

A T A RECENT charity dinner that I attended, not a lot of thought had gone into the seating plan. Or so I thought. The event had two long rectangular tables for dinner, so the people seated at the end only had a person on one side of them to talk to. A nightmare scenario for an extrovert. As it so happened, I was seated next to the man who got one of the end spots at the table. When I expressed my concern to him that he had only me to talk to, he told me not to worry about him, that he was an introvert, and that it was his idea of heaven not having to talk the whole dinner. LOL!

He was a fascinating dinner companion nonetheless with an extraordinary depth of knowledge on several subjects. This interaction reminds me of the book *Quiet: The Power of Introverts in a World That Can't Stop Talking* by Susan Cain. She argues that the West misunderstands and undervalues the traits and capabilities of introverted people, leading to "a colossal waste of talent, energy and happiness." Not everyone is gregarious, alpha and comfortable in the spotlight. And that's ok.

According to Myers Briggs' data (MBTI), the world's population is roughly split 50/50 between introverts and extroverts. Therefore, we all work and/or live with introverts. So, **Today's Take Action Tip is to make the most of your relationships with your fellow introverts.** To follow are some points to bear in mind:

- **Introverts reflect on new information at length and react relatively slowly** – They prefer not to be broadsided with big decisions or be expected to be brilliant brain-stormers without having an agenda in advance. Give them processing time to get their best ideas. Unlike extroverts who often regret what they say, introverts think before they speak so may often regret what they don't say.

- **Introverts are ok with silence** – You don't have to fill in the pauses in the conversation or finish their sentences. Quiet is ok and they are great listeners.

- **Introverts prefer to think things through** before they talk things through. Send an email first before calling or popping into their office for a chat if you are looking for feedback or a decision.

- **Introverts become de-energised by too much interaction** – They are energised by going into their inner world of ideas, thoughts and emotions and are recharged by using silence and solitude. Extroverts, by contrast, can get "cabin fever" if forced to be on their own for too long.

So, what are you going to do to benefit from your introvert relationships? Or help people value your introversion?

> *"In terms of, like, instant relief, cancelling plans is like heroin."*
>
> — John Mulaney

ASK YOURSELF, "HOW CAN I GET THE MOST OUT OF THE INTROVERTS AROUND ME?"

#Clarity #Influence #ConnectionEnergy #SpaceEnergy

Take Action Tip 17

Stop Letting Others Annoy You

"Everything that irritates us about others can lead us to an understanding of ourselves."

— Carl Jung

I n my experience, one gets annoyed by others for one of three main reasons:

1) The "annoyer" has a different model of the world from you. The way they create meaning from what they see, think and hear is completely different from the way you do.

2) What annoys you about them is really something that annoys you about yourself – which is why you noticed the offending behaviour/attitude in the first place. What you think about and focus on the most, you attract more of into your life.

3) They are just plain annoying, displaying anti-social behaviour (more often than not, resulting from no. 1 or no. 2 above).

So, do you know someone who is annoying? If so, **Today's Take Action Tip is to stop allowing others to annoy you.** Let it go. There is too much cortisol in the world! We have all learned by now that we can't change other people...so take a moment for self-reflection and to consider the following points:

- **Realise that annoying people are inevitable** – and they are not all personally out to get you! 9/10 times, it's not about you.

- **Accept that you're not a mind-reader** – If you don't understand their behaviour, be curious in a non-judgemental way instead of making up stories in your head.

- **How are you seeing yourself in that person?** – Do they have a quality you (un)consciously dislike about yourself? Maybe try to sort yourself out first?

- **Reframe your interaction** – Try assuming they are doing the best they can with the (limited) skills and awareness they have.

- **Know that getting more annoyed will not make them stop any sooner** – If all else fails, change your focus, location, body language, breath, put on headphones, de-friend, un-follow, etc., until the urge to *react* passes and you can choose a constructive *action*.

"Whenever you are about to find fault with someone, ask yourself the following question: What fault of mine most nearly resembles the one I am about to criticize?"

— Marcus Aurelius, *Meditation*

Ask Yourself, "Which Fresh Approach Can I Use To Deal With A 'Tricky' Person?"

#Courage #Influence #ConnectionEnergy #MindEnergy

Take Action Tip 18

Get to Know Some Inspiring Women

ACH YEAR, IN honour of International Women's Day, I like to share inspirational quotes from women. Even though it may not be IWD today, my **Take Action Tip is to get to know some inspiring women** (past and present). Attend conferences, join a local meet-up, watch some TEDtalks and/or read some nonfiction. It is a lot easier to learn from other people's experiences and struggles.

Below are a few quotes by wise women that have inspired me...I think you will find they are equally relevant for both men and women.

On Intuition:

> *"Follow your instincts – that's where true wisdom manifests itself."*

> — Oprah Winfrey

On Confidence:

> *"No one can make you feel inferior without your consent."*

> — Eleanor Roosevelt

On taking risks vs. playing it safe:

"Security is mostly a superstition. It does not exist in nature, nor do the children of men as a whole experience it. Avoiding danger is no safer in the long run than outright exposure. Life is either a daring adventure, or nothing."

— Helen Keller

On growing your network:

"People will forget what you said. People will forget what you did. But people will never forget how you made them feel."

— Mary Angelou

On believing in yourself:

"I know God will not give me anything I can't handle. I just wish that He didn't trust me so much."

— Mother Teresa

On gratitude:

"I don't think of all the misery but of the beauty that still remains."

— Anne Frank

On bravery:

"As we are liberated from our own fear, our presence automatically liberates others."

— Marianne Williamson

On Prioritising:

"No one ever died from sleeping in an unmade bed."

— Erma Bombeck

On taking action:

"The most effective way to do it, is to do it."

— Amelia Earhart

So, who are you inspired by? Do any of those speak to you?

ASK YOURSELF, "WHICH WORDS AND ACTIONS OF SUCCESSFUL WOMEN CAN I MODEL TO HELP ME CREATE SHORTCUTS TO MY GOALS?"

#Clarity #Influence #MindEnergy #ConnectionEnergy

TAKE ACTION TIP 19

MAKE SOME EASY HEALTH CHOICES

I HAVE HAD the good fortune to get a ticket to the Royal Geographical Society in London to listen to Dr. Deepak Chopra talk about his new book *Super Genes* that he co-authored with Rudoph Tanzi, Professor of Neurology at Harvard.

The biggest takeaway for me as a holistic executive coach was: **"Only 5% of disease-related gene mutations are fully deterministic, while 95% can be influenced by diet, behavior, and other environmental conditions."** I.e, our genes are a predisposition, but they are not our fate. Our genes respond to everything we think, say and do, so gene activity is largely under our control. **For radical well-being, we just need to start by making** easy **lifestyle choices.** None of Deepak's recommendations, taken in isolation, were radical or difficult – but when advice is easy and intuitive, it is just as easy to say, "yeah, I know" and *not* take it.

So, **Today's Take Action Tip is to commit to some easy choices to improve your health and well-being.** Start with one easy commitment in each of the six main categories that scientifically demonstrate benefit and then go ahead and make some more easy choices as habits are formed:

1) **Diet:** *Get rid of inflammation.* E.g., add prebiotics like oats for breakfast, have probiotic (fermented) foods once a day (e.g.,

kefir, active yogurt, sauerkraut) and eat a side salad with lunch and dinner.

2) **Stress:** *Keep adrenaline and cortisol in check.* E.g., avoid multi-tasking, avoid people who are sources of conflict and leave work on time at least 3 times per week.

3) **Exercise:** *Move more!* E.g., get up and move around once an hour, take a walk after dinner and take the stairs. Your lymph system detoxifies your body by movement.

4) **Meditation:** *Make it daily practice.* Sit for 10 mins with eyes closed at lunch, use a mindful technique several times a day and use a simple 10 in/out breath meditation before you go to bed.

5) **Sleep:** *Make sure you get a minimum of 7 hrs.* E.g., before bedtime, take a relaxing walk, have a warm bath and turn off devices.

6) **Emotions:** *Don't allow your emotional state to drift.* E.g., keep a gratitude journal, appreciate someone each day and spend more time with happy people.

Get consistent with some easy choices and then harder choices will become more achievable. Building a foundation of healthy choices won't just help your genes – it's also a recipe for holistic personal and professional health.

So, which easy success habits can you start forming today?

> *"Have patience. All things are difficult before they become easy."*

— Saadi

Ask Yourself, "What Is One Thing I Can Do Today To Increase My Self-Care?"

#Clarity #Energy #InputEnergy #MoveEnergy #MindEnergy #PauseEnergy #ConnectionEnergy

TAKE ACTION TIP 20

MEASURE YOUR PROGRESS

"Evaluate what you want – because what gets measured gets produced."

— James A. Belasco

ARE YOU FEELING like the glass is half-full and that you are making some great progress on your be/have/do intentions or are they on a scrap of paper suffocating somewhere under a pile of clutter where you jotted them down months ago?

Today's Take Action Tip is to take a moment for a measure and to evaluate what could bring you better results going forward (regardless of your progress so far).

A few things to bring attention to, evaluate and measure are your:

- **Levels of interference** – If an activity is sucking time and energy and not bringing you any closer to where you want to be, consider stopping it. Success = Potential – Interference (Is your interference Facebook? Interaction with someone? A bad habit?).

- **Focus** – Attention is one of your most important assets – are you investing it wisely? Are you putting it towards your purpose and passions? (Do you even know what they are?)

- **Multi-tasking** – Remember the Pareto Principle? 80% of your results come from 20% of your efforts.

- **State of health** – If not for yourself, consider how your greater energy and focus could benefit your friends, family, clients and work colleagues.

- **Levels of Concentration** – Apparently, like yawning, it is contagious. Yes, it has been proven that you can "catch" concentration. So, if you are easily distracted, set yourself up next to someone who is concentrating.

So, what do you need to measure to start living up to your potential?

"Experience doesn't make you wiser – evaluated experience makes you wiser."

— Andy Stanley

ASK YOURSELF, "WHAT IS ONE THING I CAN START MEASURING TODAY FOR GREATER SUCCESS?"

#Clarity #Productivity #Energy #MindEnergy #ConnectionEnergy

Take Action Tip 21

Be Anything but Average

"Great minds discuss ideas. Average minds discuss events. Small minds discuss people."

— Eleanor Roosevelt

THE DIFFERENCE BETWEEN ordinary and extraordinary is wafer thin. Extraordinary people go the extra mile, ordinary people do what is required. So often we diminish our energy, light and core genius with little acts of unconscious self-sabotage; "acts of average." So, **Today's Take Action Tip is to ask yourself, "Where am I unnecessarily average?"** Then choose one act of average to eliminate.

Are you:

- Late versus early?
- Self-absorbed versus self-aware?
- Sitting versus moving?
- Taking versus giving?
- Worrying versus meditating?
- Talking versus listening?

- Being busy versus productive?
- Fearing versus loving?
- Scrolling versus sleeping?
- Giving up versus persisting?
- Dehydrating versus drinking (water!)?
- Multi-tasking versus focusing?
- Blaming versus taking responsibility?
- Criticising versus appreciating?
- Gossiping versus inspiring?
- Eating processed versus clean?

If you do what most people do, you will get the results that most people get.

"There are no traffic jams along the extra mile."

— Roger Staubach

ASK YOURSELF, "WHAT IS ONE THING I CAN START MEASURING TODAY FOR GREATER SUCCESS?"

#Clarity #Productivity #Energy #MindEnergy #ConnectionEnergy

Take Action Tip 22

Bring the Energy

"The higher your energy level, the more efficient your body, the better you feel and the more you will use your talent to produce outstanding results."

— Tony Robbins

ENERGY. FOCUS. PRODUCTIVITY.

Raise your hand if you could use more of those things in your life. If you are like most people, energy is probably near the top of your "like-to-have-more-of" list.

Aside from reaching for a cup of coffee (a cup – not Grande – of java made with organic beans and without the sugar and syrup does indeed have proven health benefits), what sort of energy-boosting strategies do you have?

If you are drawing a blank, **Today's Take Action Tip is to analyse your energy "drillers" and "fillers."** What is drilling holes into your pot of energy and what is filling it up? To follow are some of my favourite (mostly quick) energisers:

- **Sleep:** 7-9 hours. Yes. Really.

- **Bone Broth:** Contains peak performance-fuelling electrolytes: potassium, calcium, magnesium and sodium – critical for allowing cells to generate energy. Email me if you want my recipe.

- **Water:** Drink 4% of your kg body weight in litres each day. Lack of water is the #1 trigger of daytime fatigue – water delivers the oxygen in your blood to all of the cells. A mere 2% drop in body water can trigger fuzzy short-term memory, trouble with basic math, and difficulty focusing on the computer screen or on a printed page.

- **Chi gong (Qigong):** The literal Chinese translation is "Life Energy Cultivation"; it is a holistic system of co-ordinated body posture and movement, breathing, and meditation. My favourite is the "chop and bounce." Close your eyes (vision is our most oxygen intensive bodily function), breathe deeply in through your nose and out through your mouth 20 times while doing karate hand chopping motions and short bouncy squats.

- **Joy:** Doing what you love and being with people you love is energising. Who is your energy angel?

- **Wheat grass:** Have a freshly squeezed shot – this chlorophyll powerhouse increases the oxygen in your blood and is a better "pick me up" or cure for hangovers than coffee.

- **7-min workout:** Some movement is always better than none. (Google 7-minute-workout. There are a many.) Sitting is the new smoking.

Energy affects everything we do—from how we show up at work to how we conduct our personal relationships.

What are your favourite energisers? I'd love to hear.

"Energy is more valuable than intelligence."

— Robin Sharma

Ask Yourself, "What Is One Thing I Can Do To Top Up My Energy?"

#Clarity #Energy #InputEnergy #MindEnergy #ConnectionEnergy #MoveEnergy

Take Action Tip 23

Be Consistent

"People are always looking for the single magic bullet that will totally change everything. There is no single magic bullet."

— Temple Grandin

OVERNIGHT SUCCESS IS a myth. Yet, at the beginning of the year, "quick fixes" for everything from diet to debt are pushed. Successful people know that **making small continual improvements every day will be compounded over time** and give them the results they seek.

I saw a picture of the billionaire Jon Butcher at age 29 and 49 – and he looked just the same. In his interview, he had no "magic bullet" (aka. easy short cut) to recommend in order to replicate his results. Just consistently eating well and working out 5 days a week. When I was at the global *The Truth About Cancer* conference in Texas in 2016, it was reiterated again and again by experts that there was no silver bullet (like chemo) to cure cancer. Again, it is a matter of taking as many consistent actions as possible that are known to improve your immune system.

So, **Today's Take Action Tip is to make your own magic by being consistent.** Look at the big areas of your life and instead of counting on one big change to be the panacea, brainstorm five small things you can do consistently that will put you on the road to success. Look at your:

- Relationships
- Health
- Finances
- Career
- Spirituality
- Growth/Intellect
- Character

What small consistent changes can you start making now to transform these areas of your life?

"Every day, in every way, I'm getting better and better."

— Emile Coue

ASK YOURSELF, "WHAT IS ONE THING I CAN START DOING TODAY, CONSISTENTLY, TO UP-LEVEL MY LIFE?"

―――――――――――――

#Clarity #Energy #Productivity #Courage #Influence #InputEnergy #MindEnergy #ConnectionEnergy #MoveEnergy #SpaceEnergy #PauseEnergy

Take Action Tip 24

Build your "No" repertoire

"It is only by saying 'No' that you can concentrate on the things that are really important.

— Steve Jobs

THE EXERCISE IN my "Conquering Overwhelm Masterclass" that I always get the most feedback on is the "No" exercise. Saying "No" is sometimes just plain tricky!

Giving our time and attention away freely, without enough push-back, is one of the main reasons we get overwhelmed. Reasons why we don't say "no" more often range from lack of focus and feeling guilty to wanting to be perceived as a team player. But the one reason for not saying "No" that I want to focus on today is "not wanting to appear rude."

Saying "No" with grace and humour is a skill that needs to be developed and honed, so **Today's Take Action Tip is to build your "No" repertoire.** Say "No" to something today – and practice a different way of saying "No" every day this week. To get started, one formula you might find helpful is the following:

1) Affirm the relationship, e.g., "It's great to hear from you."

2) Thank the person sincerely for the opportunity, e.g., "Thank you so much for thinking of me! It sounds like such a brilliant project. I'm flattered that you thought of me."

3) Decline firmly and politely, e.g., "For a number of reasons I will need to pass on this at the moment."

Your "No" should be truthful, firm, and not overly apologetic or explanatory (my particular weakness!). You may want to start building your "No" muscle first by responding to less important email requests – this is often simpler as you don't have to think on your toes. Three other phrases you may want to add to your "no" repertoire include:

- "I'd love to, but can't this week/month/year."
- "Sounds great, but I can't commit at this time."
- "I won't be able to help. If only I had a clone!"

So, what are you going to say "No" to today? Do you have any other ways for saying "No" you'd like to share? I'd love to hear how it goes – drop me a line and let me know!

"When you say 'Yes' to others, make sure you are not saying 'No' to yourself."

— Paulo Coelho

ASK YOURSELF, "WHAT IS SOMETHING GOOD I CAN SAY 'NO' TO TODAY TO MAKE ROOM FOR SAYING 'YES' TO SOMETHING GREAT?"

#Clarity #Productivity #Courage #Influence #MindEnergy #ConnectionEnergy

Take Action Tip 25

Live like a Centenarian

"Energy is more valuable than intelligence."

— Robin Sharma

ONLY ONCE, SINCE I started my weekly TATT blog-ette, did I miss one. Unfortunately, in April 2017, I had a bit of a "Code Blue" and almost met my maker due to blood poisoning. During my joy-filled 8-day hospital stay, I came across some research by *National Geographic* Fellow, Dan Buettner, on what he coined, "The Blue Zones" – areas in the world where people live the longest and are the healthiest. As a holistic executive coach, I am always interested in how productivity and success are linked to energy/health. Feel better, do better.

So, **Today's Take Action Tip is to adopt some "blue zone behaviours" to keep any "code blue" at bay:**

What, exactly, are blue zone behaviours, you ask? To follow are some of the things that people do who have the longest and healthiest lives:

Move naturally: Throughout their day as a matter of course without thinking about it. Do not stay glued to your office chair!

Have a purpose: According to the research, it's worth up to 7 years of extra life expectancy. Our day job is also more enjoyable if we can find purpose in what we do.

Slow down and deal with stress: Have a routine way of dealing with it, like meditating, napping or getting together with friends.

Eat less: Stop eating when you are 80% full.

Eat mainly plants: "Whole foods" rather than processed foods. Beans are a cornerstone of many of their diets. Get to like your veggies!

Drink in moderation or not at all: 1 to 2 glasses of red wine per day, often with a meal and with friends. But never to excess.

Have faith: Almost all centenarians interviewed belonged to some faith-based community.

Put family first: Keep ageing parents and grandparents nearby and invest in children with time and love.

Be social: Join or create supportive social circles.

So how *blue* can you be today?

"It's paradoxical, that the idea of living a long life appeals to everyone, but the idea of getting old appeals to no one."

— Andy Rooney

Ask Yourself, "What Action Can I Take Today To Increase My Longevity?"

#Clarity #Energy #Productivity #Courage #Influence #InputEnergy #MindEnergy #ConnectionEnergy #MoveEnergy #SpaceEnergy #PauseEnergy

Take Action Tip 26

De-Clutter

"Simplicity is the ultimate sophistication"

— Leonardo di Vinci

O NE OF MY ongoing life themes is de-cluttering. I throw away or donate something nearly every week and I must confess it is becoming somewhat of an addiction. With the all too frequent sightings of plastic garbage bags, my poor children have now started hiding their toys from me!

Since everything is energy, and energy needs to flow freely, by filling your environment with clutter, and by refusing to part with the things that no longer serve you, you create a lot of stagnant energy in your environment and can get, simply put, "stuck." The word "clutter" derives from the Middle English word "clotter," which means to coagulate – and that's about as stuck as you can get!

So, **Today's Take Action Tip is to become "unstuck" and take 10 minutes today to de-clutter.** Where has clutter been chipping away at your energy and now become an enemy of focus, productivity and happiness? Is it your office desk? Your kitchen? Your closet? Bear in mind it may not even be physical clutter.

Consider the following harbourers of "clutter":

Your inbox - what can you delete or unsubscribe from?

Relationships – which toxic relationship or grudges can you let go of?

Your calendar – which meetings and time zappers can you cancel or, better yet, say "no" to?

Your mind – what are your limiting beliefs and habitual unhealthy thoughts?

Noise - can you turn those annoying email alerts off already?

Go ahead and do some ditching, donating and deleting today.

"A man is rich in proportion to the number of things which he can afford to let alone."

— Henry David Thoreau

ASK YOURSELF, "WHERE IS ONE AREA IN MY LIFE - PHYSICAL OR METAPHORICAL - WHERE I CAN LET GO OF SOME CLUTTER?"

———

#Clarity #Productivity #MindEnergy #ConnectionEnergy #SpaceEnergy

TAKE ACTION TIP 27

KEEP A JOURNAL

"Follow effective action with quiet reflection. From the quiet reflection will come even more effective action"

— Peter Drucker

WRITING IS A powerful tool for self-improvement. It focuses us on our successes, helps us learn from our mistakes and makes life feel more controllable. So, **Today's Take Action Tip is to try journaling.**

Studies have shown the benefits from journaling include bringing about a state of mindfulness, increased IQ and EQ, greater goal achievement, a boost to memory and comprehension, greater self-discipline, improved communication skills, improved immune function (google Dr. James Pennebaker), more self-confidence and greater creativity. Not to mention the joy that comes with the empty pages of a beautiful new journal (I personally love www.browncow.london).

Not sure what to write about? Here are some questions to choose from:

- What went well today and why?
- What did I learn today?
- What are 3 new things I am grateful for today?

- How would I like to show up and what sort of emotions do I want to experience today?

- What do I most want to remember about today 30 days from now?

- What is the best thing that happened to me today?

- What did I love about myself today?

- What are my next top 5 priority actions?

You can do this as part of a morning ritual or before you go to bed at night. Whatever works best for you!

> *"The ideas can come from anywhere and at any time. The problem with making mental notes is that the ink fades very rapidly"*

> — Rolf Smith

ASK YOURSELF, "WHAT IS ONE THING I CAN WRITE IN MY JOURNAL TODAY TO BRING GREATER CLARITY, CONFIDENCE, PRODUCTIVITY OR GRATITUDE TO MY LIFE?"

———————————————

#Clarity #Productivity #Courage #MindEnergy

Take Action Tip 28

Develop Your Empathy

"When you show deep empathy toward others, their defensive energy goes down, and positive energy replaces it. That's when you can get more creative in solving problems."

— Stephen Covey

EMPATHY - THE ability to recognize and share other people's feelings - **can be one of the most important instruments in your toolbox as a leader.** It is particularly helpful during confrontation and disagreements.

A few years ago, my son was proudly sporting his newly acquired Spiderman suit that he got for his birthday – complete with padded, fake muscly arms. When we met up with his friend Freddy for a play-date, I saw him cast his eyes over my son's costume and immediately go green with envy. "I hate Spiderman," he said. I braced myself to mediate a mini-brawl, but instead of responding to Freddy's provocation, to my amazement, my son responded with empathy to his need and replied, "Don't worry Freddy, I'll get you a Spiderman costume for your birthday too." Freddy grinned broadly and then off they ran to play together.

Wouldn't it be great to always **have the presence of mind to respond with empathy like that when provoked, instead of retaliation?**

If you know someone who seems to have a knack for pushing your buttons, then **Today's Take Action Tip is to try practising silent empathy.**

The next time you notice a conversation becoming "difficult," to **keep calm and to prevent your emotions from hijacking your thoughts and behaviours**, try:

- **Taking a time out:** If possible, find 10 mins to take a walk or to use the restroom. Then try:
- **Imagining/guessing:** What emotional or physical needs may not be satisfied for this person that may be the cause of their intensity? Do they need appreciation, clarity, sympathy, understanding, etc?
- **Silently deliver the emotion** they require as you listen to them speak.

You don't need to be right with your guessing. **Just the act of trying to identify the needs not being satisfied will work to calm you down** and keep you from getting angry. It can help you to focus on them and empathise with them as a person with their own needs and stresses and not as someone who is trying to upset you.

You know they just want a Spiderman suit too. (Imagine them in one if it helps.)

"The opposite of anger isn't calmness, its empathy"

— Mehmet Oz

ASK YOURSELF, "WHO IS SOMEONE IN MY CIRCLE OF INFLUENCE THAT NEEDS SOME SILENT EMPATHY TODAY?"

#Clarity #Courage #Influence #MindEnergy #ConnectionEnergy

TAKE ACTION TIP 29

MASTER GAME-
CHANGING EVENTS

"It is not the mountain we conquer but ourselves."

— Edmund Hillary

Most of us, at some point, face events (interviews, pitches, key conversations, presentations) in our personal and professional lives that have the potential to be game-changers – to have a significant impact on our happiness and/or success.

The problem is, as soon as we recognise this, fear (of failure, of success, looking stupid, etc., whatever your pattern is) can kick in and subconscious, self-sabotaging, bad habits often follow.

Stop that!

So, **Today's Take Action Tip is to give up on self-limiting thoughts and behaviours to make your next big event a game-changer.**

Give up:

- **Letting your past dictate your future** – Let past failures be feedback, not your destiny.

- **Hanging out with dream-stealers** – If you are trying to get ready for a big event, don't talk it through with the crazy-makers in your life. You know who they are.

- **Trying to figure it out on your own** – Don't reinvent the wheel. Be willing to ask for advice and benefit from others' experience.

- **Multi-tasking** – unless you want to waste time, be unproductive and procrastinate all at once! *Pretending to listen* when you're really thinking about what to say next is also multi-tasking.

- **Picturing what you** don't want **instead of what you** do **want** – Instead of envisaging in Technicolour detail exactly how it will all go horribly wrong, make a clear picture in your head of how you do want it to go, like elite athletes running the race in their heads first.

So, what can you give up today to give it your all and make your next big event a game changer?

> *"Whatever you can do or dream you can, begin it. Boldness has beauty, power, and magic in it."*

> — Goethe

ASK YOURSELF, "WHICH UPCOMING EVENT CAN I PLAN TO MAKE A GAME-CHANGER?"

#Clarity #Courage #MindEnergy #ConnectionEnergy

TAKE ACTION TIP 30

GET A GREEN SHOT

"*To keep the body in good health is a duty...otherwise we shall not be able to keep our mind strong and clear.*"

— Buddha

IF YOU WANT to achieve your goals and make amazing stuff happen in your life, you need to make sure first and foremost that you are keeping your gut, a.k.a. your second brain (see link below) and the heart of your immune system, healthy. Changes in the Western diet over the past century have resulted in skyrocketing of the incidence of ailments such as diabetes, irritable bowel disease, and immune disorders as well as depression and anxiety as our diet has turned more to highly processed foods devoid of the kinds of bacteria and enzymes our bodies and brains have relied on throughout history.

Helping my Dad through his chemotherapy a few years ago, it was a stark reminder that without your health, the quality of your life and what you can achieve is limited.

While I was visiting to help out, I got my parents in the habit of drinking a one-ounce wheatgrass shot every morning. Wheatgrass juice is an effective healer because it contains all minerals known to man, and vitamins A, B-complex, C, E, l and K. It is extremely rich in protein, and contains 17 amino acids, the building blocks of protein. For 49 other reasons to drink wheatgrass (it is gluten-free, by the way), see link below.

So, **Today's Take Action Tip is to go get yourself a wheatgrass shot from your local juice bar and drink it (preferably on an empty stomach) 15 mins before eating anything.**

You could even grow your own (simple presses are not expensive) that you can order in trays if you have the space. It is a powerful concentrated liquid nutrient. Two ounces of wheatgrass juice has the nutritional equivalent of five pounds of the best raw organic vegetables. And because it's a powerful detoxifier of the blood and liver, you may even find it is a much better recovery option than black coffee after a big night out!

"The greatest wealth is health."

— Virgil

Useful links:

https://www.psychologytoday.com/articles/201110/your-backup-brain
http://thechalkboardmag.com/50-reasons-to-drink-wheatgrass-every-day

ASK YOURSELF, "WHERE AND WHEN CAN I FIND MYSELF A WHEATGRASS SHOT TODAY?"

#Energy #InputEnergy

Take Action Tip 31

Develop your Grit

"Continuous effort – not strength or intelligence – is the key to unlocking our potential."

— Winston Churchill

"Mummy – do you have grit?" asked my daughter one day. "Yes, I suppose I have a bit," said I modestly. "That's good – because my headmaster said that it is one of the most important things you need to succeed in life." When I asked her what it meant, she said it meant "to never give up." According to the Merriam-Webster dictionary, grit in the context of behaviour is defined as "firmness of character; indomitable spirit."

On her first day of learning to ski, after falling for about the tenth time, my daughter simply refused to get up again. This is when I cunningly deployed the, "what would your headmaster think about your grit?" tactic…to great effect. She managed to dig deep and find a bit of "get up and go" reserve and was soon on her way skiing again!

So, do you have a strategy to revive your "get up and go" when it has got up and gone? If not, **Today's Take Action Tip is to develop your grit.**

In Angela Duckwork's TEDtalk (viewed 10mil+ times), she explained her theory of why grit is a predictor of success and her take on the 5 main characteristics:

- **Courage:** in particular, it is your ability to manage fear of failure
- **Conscientiousness:** being achievement-oriented, working tirelessly, trying to do a good job and completing the task at hand
- **Long term goals and endurance:** continuous practice with an end purpose in mind
- **Resilience:** regulating emotion and bouncing back from unforeseen shocks and surprises
- **Striving for Excellence:** vs seeking the illusion of perfection

So how many characteristics do you have? What can you do to raise your "grit factor"?

"To strive, to seek, to find and not to yield."

— Alfred Lord Tennyson

ASK YOURSELF, "WHAT WOULD MOVE ME FASTEST TOWARDS SUCCESS TODAY? COURAGE, CONSCIENTIOUSNESS, ENDURANCE, RESILIENCE OR SEEKING EXCELLENCE?"

#Courage #Clarity #Productivity #MindEnergy

TAKE ACTION TIP 32

CONFIDENCE IS KEY

"Inaction breeds doubt and fear. Action breeds confidence and courage. If you want to conquer fear, do not sit at home and think about it. Go out and get busy."

— Aristotle

IN MY EXPERIENCE, accumulated over more than two decades of working in a corporate environment, **personal and executive presence is one of the most important factors determining the advancement of your career** (and can be helpful in your private life as well).

Should you disagree and be of the opinion that driving results is all that matters in business and everything else is a waste of time, then **Today's Take Action Tip is to go ahead and kill your executive presence.**

To best eradicate your Executive Presence and ensure you remain in a career cul-de-sac, **there are three main categories that you** must **get wrong: 1) Confidence 2) Self-awareness and 3) Energy.**

First, I'd now like to give you some simple strategies to undermine your confidence:

1) First impressions matter. **Don't let any good posture send out confident alpha signals** to others and *certainly* **do not invest in your wardrobe** (work clothes are a total waste of money – *why*

bother?! You only wear them about 60-70% of the time). Your clubbing or weekend walking clothes will *Do. Just. Fine.*

2) Ahead of any public speaking engagements, hyperventilate **with shallow breathing to ensure your mind goes blank from the loss of carbon dioxide.** Don't forget to also focus on the horrible things people might be thinking about you **and visualise** all **the embarrassing questions they will ask you** to guarantee you are *as-nervous-as-possible.*

3) Don't **contribute in team meetings.** Scoot as far away from the meeting table as possible to avoid involvement and take notes on your lap like a stenographer. If people look to you for answers, quickly look down or away. If you simply *can't resist* contributing to a discussion – make sure you minimise what you have to say by apologising for interrupting with *"Sorry,* I *just* wanted to say…it's *probably a bad idea but…".*

4) **Don't go to** too **many networking events** – *it could, well, build you a network. But…*if you *do* – make sure that you stand in a corner with your arms folded tightly across your chest, clutching your drink to you like a weapon. If possible, also use a notebook as a shield. Beware! Casual chats *have been known to kill.*

Follow these strategies closely and you can be sure to:

- Kill your *confidence*
- zap your *energy,* and
- Stymy any *promotion potential*

5) And one final piece of advice…above all, don't **get a coach!**

So, how are you going to ensure you lack confidence today?

"No one can make you feel inferior without your consent."

— Eleanor Roosevelt

ASK YOURSELF, "WHAT ACTION CAN I TAKE TO INCREASE MY EXECUTIVE PRESENCE AND SELF-AWARENESS TODAY?"

#Courage #Clarity #influence #Productivity #MindEnergy #MoveEnergy #ConnectionEnergy

TAKE ACTION TIP 33

BECOME SELF-AWARE

"I think self-awareness is probably the most important thing towards being a champion"

— Billie Jean King

IN MY EXPERIENCE, accumulated over more than two decades of working in a corporate environment, **personal and executive presence is one of the most important factors determining the advancement of your career** (and can be helpful in your private life as well).

Should you disagree and be of the opinion that driving results is all that matters in business and everything else is a waste of time, then **Today's Take Action Tip is to go ahead and kill your executive presence.**

To best eradicate your Executive Presence and ensure you remain in a career cul-de-sac, **there are three main categories that you** must **get wrong: 1) Confidence 2) Self-awareness and 3) Energy.**

Today, in Part 2, I'd like to start by giving you some strategies to prevent any development of Self-awareness:

Do assume your boss knows all the good things you are up to. Don't waste her time sharing your wins and updates…she has telepathic powers. Of course.

Under no circumstances ask for feedback on your performance. Feedback-means-failure. Discourage your boss and others from giving it by getting angry and reacting defensively…or cry.

When confronted about poor decisions or errors you've made, do not take responsibility! Admit nothing, deny everything and make counter accusations…or cry.

Be seen to be complaining and gossiping whenever possible. Channel that inner energy vampire to suck the motivation out of those around you.

When colleagues come to seek your counsel, just nod your head and pretend to listen. No need to make eye contact or to try to read between the lines.

Seek to win arguments at all costs and be quick to point out others' faulty logic. Don't settle for merely being right. Make others wrong.

And when it comes to the holidays, ignore received wisdom that "no one ever got promoted off the back of the Christmas party." Down a few shots, let your hair down and show them your inner tramp with your sexy dance moves…and then call in sick the next day for good measure.

So, how are you going to ensure your lack of self-awareness?

"The worse a person is, the less he feels it."

— Seneca the Younger

ASK YOURSELF, "WHAT ACTION CAN I TAKE TO INCREASE MY EXECUTIVE PRESENCE AND SELF-AWARENESS TODAY?"

#Courage #Clarity #Influence #ConnectionEnergy

Take Action Tip 34

—— ❦ ——

Power Up

"The energy of the mind is the essence of life."

— Aristotle

IN MY EXPERIENCE, accumulated over more than two decades of working in a corporate environment, **personal and executive presence is one of the most important factors determining the advancement of your career** (and can be helpful in your private life as well).

Should you disagree and be of the opinion that driving results is all that matters in business and everything else is a waste of time, then **Today's Take Action Tip is to go ahead and kill your executive presence.**

To best eradicate your Executive Presence and ensure you remain in a career cul-de-sac, **there are three main categories that you** must **get wrong: 1) Confidence 2) Self-awareness and 3) Energy.**

Today, in Part 3, I'd now like to give you some simple strategies to drain your energy and kill your charisma.

1) **No matter how unproductive or tired you are – Remain seated!** – Moving for regular breaks may just prove too refreshing and stimulate your creative thinking.

2) **At lunchtime, make sure you grab a high sugar/high carb meal to eat at your desk** – Fizzy drinks and pre-packaged san-

dwiches with processed meats are *purr*fect. This will help you write off any possible afternoon productivity with a food-induced coma.

3) **Don't meditate or practice mindfulness** – Let your stress hormones go wild to raise your chances of irrational outbursts, dulled decision-making and overall burnout.

4) **Keep your desk as cluttered as possible** – to constantly remind yourself of your workload and to keep people waiting as you dig for important documents.

5) **A good night's sleep? Are you kidding?** – You'll have time for sleeping *When. You. Are. Dead!*

So, how are you going to ensure you lack energy today?

"Energy and persistence conquer all things."

— Benjamin Franklin

ASK YOURSELF, "WHAT ACTION CAN I TAKE TO INCREASE MY EXECUTIVE PRESENCE, ENERGY AND CHARISMA TODAY?"

#Energy #MoveEnergy #InputEnergy #PauseEnergy #SpaceEnergy

TAKE ACTION TIP 35

MAKE SPACE

L ET'S TALK TODAY about Space. Not the final frontier…but the Space immediately surrounding you. As I elaborated on earlier, one of your key energy sources comes from your "Space." *Space* energy is the energy you get (or leak) from exposure to the material objects and environments you choose to surround yourself with.

So, **Today's Take Action Tip is to sort out your space.**

Life has enough complexities without clutter creating confusion and adding fuel to the chaotic fire. **When you clear things out** – whether it's a wallet, a drawer, your car, the closet, your desk, or even the refrigerator – **you are clearing energy that is stuck and creating space for something new.** If not, you can get so busy dodging the debris that your vision becomes clouded. How could you possibly have the energy to tackle important complex issues when you can't even find a pair of scissors when you need to?

Other things to consider in your space that can add or subtract from your energy:

- Do your clothes and shoes fit well and feel good (including your undergarments, ladies)?

- What sort of background sounds or music are you loving or tolerating?

- Is your bed and home comfortable, your workspace ergonomic?

- Is your work and living space surrounded by objects, photos, words or views that inspire?

- How's your email inbox looking?

- Do you have a special place to relax and unwind?

- How much contact do you have with nature?

- What sort of scents/fresh air/smells are you breathing in?

Bring awareness to your surroundings. Allowing uncomfortable clothes and furniture, clutter, distracting smells, sights and sounds, excess digital stimulation, etc., into your space can energetically chip away at you and contribute to overwhelm.

Lose the litter of your landscape and watch how your energy rises!

ASK YOURSELF, "WHAT'S ONE ACTION I CAN TAKE TODAY TO SPRUCE UP MY SPACE AND IMPROVE MY ENERGY?"

#Clarity #Productivity #SpaceEnergy

TAKE ACTION TIP 36

BE COURAGEOUSLY AUTHENTIC

WHEN I SPEAK about the courage to be your authentic self in all areas of your life, I use the acronym SW4. For my London readers, you may be forgiven for thinking that **SW4** was referring to the post code of Lambeth. Or the music festival on Clapham Common. But I am actually referring to an attitude of authenticity. The courage and confidence to be, show and value the real you. SW4 is recognising that if you do…

1) **Some Will**…like you, value your ideas, want to hire you, etc., and…

2) **Some Won't.** Not everyone will value your gifts.

3) **So What?** Who cares?! Don't waste your energy trying to be someone you're not.

4) **Someone's Waiting**…that does.

So, **Today's Take Action Tip is to have the courage to be yourself** – everyone else is taken. "Authenticity," as defined by psychologists Brian Goldman and Michael Kernis, is "the unimpeded operation of one's true or core self in one's daily enterprise."

Just be you! The world needs your unique strengths. You are enough (imperfect as you are). (**Some Will** value that.)

Trying to be a clone of someone else, or someone you're expected to be, won't work. If your goal is to please everyone, you'll always fall short; you'll never make everyone happy. (**Some Won't** like or "get" you.)

Don't let others' judgments of your dreams and goals drown out your hope. What people think of you seldom has anything to do with who you are. It has everything to do with who they are. People are projecting all the time. (**So What?**)

Don't let your innermost spark, the passion that ignites you, die. You are one of a kind and have a purpose only you can fulfil. Don't waste precious time and energy trying to convince others that you are or aren't what they think you are. If they like you - that's fine. If they don't - then that's fine too…because you do know out there, **Someone's Waiting.**Get clear on what you care about, trust your intuition and be willing to reveal essential aspects of yourself with others.

So, **how are you going to be courageously true to yourself?**

"Your time is limited, so don't waste it living someone else's life."

— Steve Jobs

ASK YOURSELF, "WHAT IS ONE ACTION I CAN TAKE TODAY TO LIVE CONGRUENTLY WITH MY VALUES AND PASSIONS?"

———

#Clarity #Courage #MindEnergy #ConnectionEnergy

Take Action Tip 37

Get Along with People

"Success in life, in anything, depends upon the number of persons that one can make himself agreeable to."

— Thomas Carlyle

EVERYTHING IS ENERGY. **And the more you have, the greater the results you can create in your personal and professional life.** One of the most important sources of energy comes from positive connection to others.

In nearly all coaching relationships, at some point the conversation will turn to dysfunctional relationships. Relationships can boost your energy (when you feel seen, heard and appreciated) but also drain it away when connection is poor. Frequent scenarios causing "energy leaks" feature office politics, bad bosses, demotivated employees, poor customer service, uncooperative colleagues, demanding children and bickering spouses. Do any of these scenarios sound familiar?

If so, **Today's Take Action Tip is to maximise your connection energy.** Write down the 5-10 people you interact the most with in a given week. Next, put a '+' or '–' beside each name according to whether interaction with them tends to bring you up or down energetically. Then tell them frankly how they ranked. (Just Kidding!) Start by choosing the person on your list with a '–' with whom a better relationship would result in the biggest overall positive impact on your energy. The goal is to improve your connection with them. **Understanding you can't change other people is key to improving connection**. We all have a different model of the world based on our culture, upbringing and belief system. All you can do is choose different ways to *act* yourself (words, thoughts, tone, behaviour) and as a result, you are likely to get different *reactions*.

4 things to consider about the person/people you'd like better connection with:

- **How do they like to take in information?** Do they prefer practical detail and current specifics or are they big picture and future oriented?

- **Do they tend to make decisions prioritising** feelings and people? Or, dispassionately looking at the logical pros and cons?

- **Do you get their most considered thoughts** by giving them time to think and communicating via email or by approaching them for a face-to-face chat or brainstorm?

- **Do they work and live** preferring structure and linear planning or spontaneously and thriving on last minute options?

Notice any differences in your preferences? Now, consider what might happen if you were to tweak your communication and actions to accommodate their preferences. Go on, it's worth a try!

> *"The most important single ingredient in the formula of success is the knack of getting along people."*

> — Theodore Roosevelt

Ask Yourself, "What Is One Tweak I Can Make To My Behavior Today To Elicit A Better Response From A Person In My Circle Of Influence?"

#Clarity #Courage #influence #MindEnergy #ConnectionEnergy

Take Action Tip 38

Get Hydrated

"In wine there is wisdom, in beer there is freedom, in water there is bacteria."

— Benjamin Franklin

7 5% of Americans are chronically dehydrated. In 37% of Americans, the thirst mechanism is so weak that it is mistaken for hunger. (Hello obesity epidemic). 5% **dehydration = 20% less brain function.** And even MILD dehydration can slow metabolism down by as much as 3%. Busy people are often dehydrated people. A mere 2% drop in body water can trigger fuzzy short-term memory, trouble with basic math, and difficulty focusing on the computer screen or on a printed page. Ever experience that? With the race to get things done and tick things off your to-do list, it is easy to forget to drink enough water. If this is the case with you, I am not suggesting, as Ben Franklin did, to hydrate with beer!

Today's **Take Action Tip is to** go ahead, shock your liver and **drink some water! Pure, distilled water, that is.** Specifically, 4% of your body weight. (Note: 1 kilo = 2.2 pounds and 1 kilo of water is circa 1 litre of water.) So, if you weigh 68 kilos or about 150 lbs, you'd want to be drinking 2.7 litres of water per day (92 ounces or 11.5 8-oz glasses of water per day). More if you are working out.

Distilled water:

- **Is 100% pure water** consisting only of Hydrogen & Oxygen and NOTHING ELSE – with a TOTAL ABSENCE of any other ingredients or contaminants.

- Is absolutely clean and pure when it enters our body, so it **is free to absorb and wash away the poisons** our system generates – which is why it's called *the universal solvent*!

- Drunk on an empty stomach, **purifies the colon, making it easier to absorb nutrients** – so drink lots when you wake up.

- **Increases the production of new blood and muscle cells** = more energy.

So, if you find greater productivity, more energy, healthy skin, a healthy heart, a better immune system and a lower cancer risk to be desirable qualities, then motivate, hydrate and feel great!

And don't listen to ole Ben Franklin above – ever seen his beer belly?!!

"Pure water is the world's first and foremost medicine."

—Slovakian Proverb!

ASK YOURSELF, "HOW CAN I MAKE SURE I AM ADEQUATELY HYDRATED TODAY?"

———————————

#Productivity #Energy #InputEnergy

Take Action Tip 39

---※---

Validate Others

"Connection is the energy that is created between people when they feel seen, heard and valued – when they can give and receive without judgement."

— Brene Brown

I ONCE READ somewhere that all bad behaviour is really just a request for love, attention and/or validation. Dealing with conflict – be it with your kids, your spouse or work colleagues – can be exhausting. Great connection is energising, but the effort it takes to prove you're "right," convince, justify and/or make the other person "wrong" is draining. Affinity trumps accuracy in interactions with others every time. By helping others meet their needs, the positive energy will flow back to you. Conflict ends when true validation begins.

Validation is communicating to another person that their thoughts, opinions, ideas, beliefs and emotions are important to you, regardless of whether you agree with them or they make sense to you. The need for validation is a universal motivator, which explains why so many of us have become addicted to our digital devices. Texts, likes, stars, etc., make validation feel more tangible so we check in every few minutes for the next dopamine rush, the next morsel of validation. No one in the real, physical world can "follow" you (it would be a bit weird) or like, favourite, repost or retweet something as you say it…but they can smile or laugh and *"Nothing is as empowering as real-world validation, even if it's for failure."* — Steven Pressfield.

So, if you want to improve your real-world connection and communication, **Today's Take Action Tip is to work on validating those around you.** Be the type of person that makes everyone you come across feel perfectly okay with being exactly who they are:

- **Compliment** people and express gratitude and appreciation.
- **Magnify their strengths** (instead of their weaknesses).
- When someone is angry or frustrated **tell them that they have every right to feel that way** (instead of "calm down").
- **Listen.** Nod and say, *"I hear you." "I see you."* Show them that what they say matters.
- **Don't debate, diminish or try to fix their feelings.** Resist the urge to control how they feel or how long they should feel it.

Everyone has the need for validation, no matter who they are.

So, who are you going to validate today?

> *"Validation doesn't mean we agree with another's subjective reality. Validation allows another person's emotional state a space to exist."*
>
> — Dr. Jamie Long

Ask Yourself, "Who Are The 5 People I Can Appreciate Or Validate Today?"

#Clarity #Courage #Influence #ConnectionEnergy

Take Action Tip 40

Implement

"Knowing is not enough. We must apply. Willing is not enough. We must do."

— Johann Wolfgang von Goethe

AT A CANCER conference I attended in 2017, where about 50 scientists, doctors and alternative health experts from around the world shared their views on how to prevent and beat cancer, I certainly learned a lot of new information. But some of the "basics" I already knew: Let food be your medicine, reduce your toxic exposure, balance your energy, heal emotional wounds, embrace biological dentistry, use therapeutic plant/herbal supplements, move your body, adopt early detection with Thermography and cutting-edge blood tests, etc. Near the end of the conference, Dr. Mercola made the observation that **it isn't the lack of knowledge now that is keeping people from getting the results they want – it's FTI. Failure to Implement.** People are simply *not* doing what they *know* they need to do.

So, if you *know* what you need to do to get to where you want to be, **Today's Take Action Tip is to** implement!

This doesn't just apply to your health. The same could be said in all areas of your life from personal to professional. **Have you accumulated the knowledge but are not following through?** If you seem to be stuck at the moment, why not:

- **Follow a tried and tested formula, plan or strategy** instead of trying to reinvent the wheel and doing it your own way? That just encourages procrastination.

- **Get a coach or learn from others' success** – You really don't have to go through experiencing everything first-hand!

- **Leverage a good system and habits** to help your implementation be more consistent.**Adopt a positive mindset** instead of allowing past experiences and beliefs to hold you back from growing.**Prioritise** instead of allowing yourself to get overwhelmed.

- **Activate the power of accountability** to encourage you to commit to taking positive action.

It is time to implement what you know and follow through on your thoughts, words and dreams with consistent, recurring action.

So, what are you going to *really know* by implementing it today?

> *"A good idea is about ten percent and implementation and hard work, and luck is 90 percent."*

— Guy Kawasaki

ASK YOURSELF, "WHERE DO I NEED TO IMPLEMENT TO 10X MY SUCCESS TODAY?"

#Clarity #Courage #MindEnergy

TAKE ACTION TIP 41

KEEP IT SIMPLE

"There is not greatness where there is no simplicity, goodness and truth."

— Leo Tolstoy

KISS IS AN acronym for "Keep it simple, stupid," a design principle noted by the U.S. Navy in 1960. The KISS principle states that most systems work best if they are kept simple, therefore, simplicity should be a key goal in design and unnecessary complexity should be avoided.

From Leonardo da Vinci's *"Simplicity is the ultimate sophistication"* to Mies Van Der Rohe's *"Less is more"* the consensus is "KISS it." So, **Today's Take Action Tip is to** KISS it!

KISS what, exactly, you ask? Well, just about anything and everything!

Here are three ways to start "KISSing" things in your life:

1) **Simplify your communication:** Form sentences with 7 words or less. Sentences ≤ 7 words achieve 95% comprehension. Practice the rule of three when presenting and avoid jargon. Keep your pitches and PowerPoint slides to 3 key points. What three things do you want them to remember?

2) **Wherever you are, be there:** Multitasking is the opposite of simple. We can't be in more than one place at the same time. If you're at dinner with your family, be at dinner with your family. Be present, be focused and be mindful.

3) **Live your purpose:** Being all things to all people is not simple. Find your purpose in the service of an idea or cause using your unique talents and capacity. Once you figure out your purpose – put all of your focus and capacity on action; less noise, less thoughts. I love the short, simple talk Guy Kawasaki did at Stanford University about creating meaning – see link below.

As you continue your day, remember: *"In character, in manner, in style, in all things the supreme excellence is simplicity."* — Henry Wadsworth Longfellow.

Useful Links:

Guy Kawasaki talk
https://www.youtube.com/watch?v=54kpwPXCyxo

ASK YOURSELF WITH EVERY TASK AND INTERACTION YOU APPROACH, "HOW CAN I MAKE THIS SIMPLE AND EASY?"

#Clarity #Productivity #MindEnergy #ConnectionEnergy

TAKE ACTION TIP 42

DO A THOUGHT AUDIT

"Very little is needed to make a happy life; it is all within yourself, in your way of thinking."

— Marcus Aurelius

IF THOUGHT BUBBLES appeared above your head, making your thoughts visible to everyone, would you be in trouble? **Our thoughts create our emotions and our emotions create our experience of life**...so what are you thinking about? Research has shown most people have about 50,000 thoughts per day, 70-80% of which are negative. And the National Science Foundation says about 95% of our thoughts are habitual. So that is a whole lot of worrying, critical, self-sabotaging negative nonsense!

Today's Take Action Tip is to do a thought audit. Set a timer today for every couple of hours and observe your thoughts. How are you thinking about yourself? How are you thinking about your friends, family and colleagues? And more importantly, **consider how your current thinking is creating your perception of reality.**

Someone who was great at auditing his thoughts was Mohammed Ali – a true master of sports psychology. He was great at thinking about what he wanted and turning his dreams into factual mantras or affirmations.

He habitually repeated "I am the greatest" and "impossible is nothing" long before he became world champion. **What are some habitual thoughts you have that could be replaced with more helpful ones?** Go ahead and jot them down every time the timer rings.

It is precisely this sort of change in thinking that I had earlier in my career that I credit with my biggest ever job promotion. I wrote about this in the book I co-authored in 2015, *Success University for Women*, available on Amazon.com.

Our body doesn't only metabolize food – it metabolizes thoughts as well. Negative thoughts are metabolized into inflammation and a stress response. Positive thoughts are metabolized into detoxification and healing. Be present to the thought choices you are making.

"There is nothing good or bad but thinking makes it so."

— William Shakespeare

ASK YOURSELF, "IS MY CURRENT THINKING AROUND THE PERSON OR SITUATION HELPING?"

#Clarity #Influence #MindEnergy #ConnectionEnergy

Take Action Tip 43

Be Grateful

"Gratitude is not only the greatest of virtues, but the parent of all others."

— Marcus Tullius Cicero

THE NAME OF the American holiday "Thanksgiving" conveys what the day is supposed to be about. It has always been my favourite holiday – the time to reflect on all I have to be grateful for and eating good food (my pumpkin pie is to die for) with close friends and family without the pressure of present-giving. But from all of the emails I get at that time of the year with the word "black" in them, you could be forgiven for thinking it is all about buying stuff. "Black Friday," the day after Thanksgiving, is historically the biggest shopping day of the year in the U.S. but has now morphed into Black Friday *week* – gone online and gone global. Poor Thanksgiving has been overshadowed by deep-discount deals on Amazon!

Given that our overly-scheduled lives often make it difficult to take a step back and spend time appreciating all that we have, **Today's Take Action Tip is to take a minute to make gratitude the "new black."** It can turn pessimism into optimism, mistakes turn into lessons, and challenges into an opportunity to grow.

Ask yourself:

- **What are 3 new things you are grateful for today?** (Try to stretch your gratitude muscle beyond friends, family and health – be specific.)

- **Who are 3 people in your life that need appreciation?** E.g., more than half of employees surveyed admit they'd stay longer at their jobs if their bosses showed more (*genuine!*) appreciation toward them.

- **Who are 3 people you can you praise or thank publicly?** (This could even be your local coffee barista!)

"Give thanks for a little and you will find a lot."

— Hansa Proverb

Useful Links:

How did Black Friday get its name? http://www.snopes.com/holidays/thanksgiving/blackfriday.asp)

ASK YOURSELF, "WHAT PEOPLE, THINGS, CHOICES, EXPERIENCES, INTERACTIONS AND THOUGHTS AM I GRATEFUL FOR TODAY?"

———————————

#Clarity #Influence #MindEnergy #ConnectionEnergy

Take Action Tip 44

Create a "Stop-Doing" list

"One half of knowing what you want is knowing what you must give up to get it."

—Sidney Howard

I DON'T KNOW about you, but around New Year, my inbox is flooded with things I should be doing. From Detoxing and dieting to setting new year's resolutions. Things we need urgently to *start* doing. But I think there is a lot to be said for a *stop doing* list.

One of my all-time favourite videos is an old skit by comedian Bob Newhart titled "Stop it." See link below.

He highlights, in a very amusing way, that you are in charge of your own thoughts, ideas and actions – no one else. So, for a better year, **Today's Take Action Tip is to think about what's currently holding you back – and then Stop It!**

To follow are some things you may want to consider stopping:

- **Trying to please everyone** – *Impossible and exhausting*
- **Demanding perfection** – *imperfect action is better than perfect procrastination*

- **Thinking you are not good enough** – *you are good enough*
- **Comparing yourself to others** – *"Comparison is the thief of joy."* — Theodore Roosevelt *(and jealousy is usually its partner in crime)*
- **Saying "yes" all the time** – *build your "no" repertoire*
- **Staying in your comfort zone** – *once you stretch out of it, you'll never go back*
- **Procrastinating on the ideas that will move you forward** – *JFDI (Just F'ing Do It!)*
- **Worrying about what others think** – *they are just doing the same thing*
- **Blaming and complaining** – *Don't be an energy vampire*
- **Overthinking** – *take action. Fail fast, fall forward*
- **Looking at your smartphone/emails first thing in the morning** – *a.k.a., the quicksand of other people's agendas*
- **Making excuses** – *Take 100% responsibility*
- **Allowing others' opinions of you to determine your reality** – *believe in yourself*
- **Thinking you have to do it all on your own** – *collaborate, delegate, get a coach!*

So, choose one thing and *stop it*!

> *"To get what you want stop doing what isn't working."*

> — Earl Warren

Useful Links:

The wonderful Bob Newhart:
https://www.youtube.com/watch?v=arPCE3zDRg4

Ask Yourself, "What Is One Thing I Need To Stop Doing Today?"

#Clarity #Influence #MindEnergy #ConnectionEnergy

Take Action Tip 45

Go Slow to Go Fast

"Celerity is never more admired than by the negligent."

— Cleopatra

EGYPTIAN QUEEN CLEOPATRA – A.K.A., philosopher, poet, orator, astronomer and speaker of 9 languages (that is a lot of talking!) – was one of history's most famous female leaders. One of her more memorable quotes (above) on celerity basically sums up the view that no one admires speed more than the lazy and negligent. The right way is *not* always the fast and easy way. I'm all for taking imperfect action over perfect procrastination, but there is also merit sometimes in not promptly pursuing the path of least resistance. These days, we work fast, talk fast, think fast, eat fast, play fast. So, **Today's Take Action Tip is to decide where you can** go slow to go fast.

- **Do you need to take time to choose, buy, prepare and mindfully consume food that will help you thrive?** (see link below)

- **Do you need to meditate?** (see link below)

- **Do you need to take the time to understand where your difficult colleague/boss/clients are coming from?** Instead of jumping to a hasty conclusion or reaction? Or wasting time constantly complaining about them?

- **Do you need to create a morning routine to help you "win" your day?** Instead of waking and rushing straight into fire-fighting and reaction mode?

- **Do you need to get clarity on a project you've been given before jumping in and executing?** Be it a family holiday or a presentation for your bosses, does their idea of success look like yours?

Reconnect with your inner tortoise as opposed to the hare! This does not mean doing everything at a snail's pace. It's about striking a balance and using your time more wisely.

So, what are you going to *do slow to go fast* today?

"I will not be triumphed over."

— Cleopatra

Useful Links:

Plant-Powered and Thriving Series https://thriving.foodrevolution.org/?orid=772991&opid=272

Try Deepak and Oprah's quarterly Free 21-Day Meditation Experience https://chopracentermeditation.com

ASK YOURSELF, "WHERE DO I NEED TO SLOW THINGS DOWN TODAY TO INCREASE MY SUCCESS?"

―――――――――――

#Clarity #Influence #MindEnergy #PauseEnergy #ConnectionEnergy #InputEnergy

Take Action Tip 46

Invest in Yourself

"Invest in as much of yourself as you can, you are your own biggest asset by far."

— Warren Buffett

In the past, I have been lucky enough to speak at one of Sheerluxe's Women's Day Conferences in London. The theme of the one that I spoke at was about investing in yourself – your happiness, your health, your career and much more. I spoke about creating your own personal energy plan, strategies to create holistic peak performance in your personal and professional life.

The problem I often see with people that are not getting the results they want in life is that they are unwilling to invest in themselves and their own energy. Their "energy pot" is empty and they are struggling to cook up anything inspiring in their lives, yet they still look outside of themselves for the solution.

So, **Today's Take Action Tip is to look at a challenge you are having and ask yourself, "Am I willing, at this time, to make the investment required to make a positive difference in this area of my life?"** If yes, then invest in yourself. If no, breathe and let it go.

To follow are just a few of the pearls of wisdom I gleaned from my fellow conference speakers:

Invest in your:

- **Communication skills** – The moments that matter most in life take place face to face – not on your laptop or iPad. Speaking beats typing every time.

- **Gut health** – Your microbiome is 100 trillion bacteria. Unhappy gut = unhappy you. Eat fresh, real food (7 portions of plants a day) and prebiotic (e.g., artichokes, apples) and probiotic (e.g., miso, kefir) foods to feed the good bacteria. Then fast for at least 12 hrs overnight.

- **Network** – We don't have enough time in life to only learn from our own mistakes – we need mentors and sponsors. Preferably, lots of them.

- **Mental health** – Meditate or practice mindfulness and get 7-9 hours of sleep. Yes, really! Six hours is simply not enough.

- **Happiness** – Be you (everyone else is taken) and follow your purpose and passions.

- **Continuing Education** – Why would you leave your personal or professional development in the hands of others? Take a course, watch a TED Talk, get a coach, etc.

So, what investment are you going to make in yourself today?

"An investment in knowledge always pays the best interest."

— Ben Franklin

Ask Yourself, "What Investment Do I Need To Make In Myself To Level Up Today?"

#Clarity #Energy #MindEnergy #PauseEnergy #ConnectionEnergy #InputEnergy

Take Action Tip 47

Go to Bed

"I have so much to do that I am going to bed."

— Old Savoyard proverb

"STAYING UP LATE to get more done" would be an oxymoron if it was a word. Too many people are tired and wired, which is not a formula for positivity and productivity. Sleep is. When sleeping, your brain gets rid of toxins, consolidates your ideas, puts short-term memory into long term and works on finding solutions. Getting some Zzzzzz's also helps with emotional regulation, decision making, hormone regulation, focus and attention. All kind of useful, n'est-ce pas?

So, **Today's Take Action Tip is simply to** go to bed. Studies show 95% of the population needs 7-9 hours of sleep per night. If you aren't getting that amount, then go to bed earlier! You are already getting up as late as you can – so the only real option is to ritualise an earlier bed time. Here are some of my top sleep "hacks":

Before bed... wind down. Turn off devices at least 30 mins beforehand, make sure your bedroom is cool, dark and electronics-free, turn on some "beta blocker" Bach chamber music or a guided sleep meditation to slow down your heart rate and breathing, brain dump your worries on a piece of paper and write down 5 new things you're grateful for. And no coffee after 3 pm, no big dinners and no alcohol two hours before bed (it messes with your Rapid Eye Movement sleep).

Go to bed… at a regular time. Your internal body clock, a mass of 20,000 clock cells found just behind your eyes, manages your sleep rhythms so go to bed and get up at roughly the same time each day. Set an alarm for 30 mins beforehand. If you need to stay up late, still get up as close to your usual time as possible to prevent disturbing your next night's sleep. About 33% of your life is spent in your bed so invest in an awesome mattress too. Don't skimp - life's too short for back aches.

Stay in bed: If you wake at night, avoid turning on the light to read, watching TV or playing with your phone. The light emitted from such electronic devices unhelpfully stimulates the light sensitive cells in your eyes, disturbing your cortisol and melatonin levels. Stay in bed in the dark and conserve your energy by lying still and being calm. Describe to yourself the duvet touching your toes and/or focus on your breathing, noticing the cool air going in your nostrils and the warm air going out to avoid night time worrying.

So, make sleep a priority today. Get an extra hour's shut-eye every day for the next week and *literally* sleep your way to the top!

"Last night I didn't sleep for a solid eight hours. No, it melted a little. Damn global warming."

— Jarod Kintz,
This Book is Not FOR SALE. ba-dum-bum-CHING.

Ask Yourself, "What Can I Do To Ensure I Get A Good Night's Rest Tonight?"

#Clarity #Energy #InputEnergy

Take Action Tip 48

Eliminate
Interference

"Performance = potential-interference, P=p-i."

— Tim Gallwey

THE QUOTE ABOVE was taken from the best-selling book *The Inner Game of Tennis* which spawned an entire series of "Inner Game" books on Work, Stress, Music, etc. According to the formula, which is applied throughout the books, performance can be enhanced either by growing "p" potential or by decreasing "i" interference.

In my quest to find out how to maximise energy, I have attended many conferences with leading health and wellness experts from around the world and have read a library full of spiritual, mental and physical health books. My biggest takeaways could easily fill a new Inner Game book! In my personal journey to heal "naturally" from cancer, something that is killing 1 in 7 people worldwide today, I have found that there is no "silver bullet" cure. But you can increase your performance (longer life) by:

Growing your potential: Exercise, eat organic, non-GMO vegetables, fruits and organic free-range meat, drink filtered water, use essential oils, do intermittent fasting, incorporate herbs and medicinal mushrooms into your diet, adopt self-love and a positive attitude, get annual thermograms, meditate, research your options and,

Decrease your interference: Eliminate sugar (cancer cells have 20x the number of insulin receptors so they feed on sugar), processed and GMO food, stress, toxic people, unnecessary antibiotics and vaccines, minimise EMF pollution (do not hold devices with a WIFI signal directly next to your body), use natural personal care and hygiene products (your skin is your largest organ), eliminate harsh chemical cleaners from your home, etc.

So, **Today's Take Action Tip is to apply P=p-i to an area of your life where you are not getting the results you want.** It could be work, your family life, your health, etc. Where is your performance being diminished by interference? Such as:

- Limiting beliefs you have?
- Poor habits you continue?
- Conflict you take part in?
- Low confidence you project?
- Distractions you allow?
- Clutter you surround yourself with?

So, how can you increase your potential and eliminate interference to get the outcomes you want?

"Nature needs no help, just no interference."

— B.J Palmer

ASK YOURSELF, "WHAT CAN I DO TO MINIMIZE INTERFERENCE TODAY?"

#Clarity #Productivity #Courage #Energy #InputEnergy #ConnectionEnergy #MindEnergy #MoveEnergy #PauseEnergy #SpaceEnergy

Take Action Tip 49

Be Decisive

"You don't need more time in your day. You need to decide."

— Seth Godin

DECISIONS, DECISIONS! **What you are and what you become depends on the decisions you make in the time that you have.** Everyone in the world is given the same amount of time. You can't stop time – but you can decide on how it is used.

Indecision is the thief of opportunity; it keeps the door closed, the opportunity waiting.

What *could* be ends up banished or postponed. Someone once told me that the universe puts expiry dates on good ideas. If you get shown a great idea and don't act on it swiftly, it gets shown to someone else. You snooze, you lose.

If you are like most people, **you have about a 5-second window to move from knowledge of what you know you** should **do (idea) into action** before your "protective," *procrastination-prone* brain kicks into full gear, sabotaging any decisions or talking you out of any timely changes of behaviour. The key is to take at least one small action, immediately, to move you in the direction of your goal or what you know you should do. E.g., Alarm goes off. Get up within 5 seconds before you hit the snooze.

Decide - commit - act - succeed - rinse and repeat.

So, **Today's Take Action Tip is to make some decisions!** Your life comes down to your decisions. When you understand that you always have the choice within 5 seconds to go from autopilot to decision maker, everything in your life can change. Your productivity will soar, and you will be better in your relationships, in your work, in the gym, everywhere. Because indecision is mainly caused by fear and you will realise the amount of rubbish you put in the way of your hopes, your dreams, your potential, your confidence and your courage.

Take extreme ownership of your thoughts and decisions. Don't blame other people or things. Take ownership of your mistakes and your problems and then take ownership of the solutions. Take ownership of your job, your future and your life. Decide and take action.

"Indecision and delays are the parents of failure."

— George Canning

ASK YOURSELF, "WHAT DECISION DO I NEED TO MAKE TODAY TO BE MORE JOYFUL, CONFIDENT AND FULLY ENGAGED?"

#Clarity #Productivity #Courage #Influence #Energy #MindEnergy #ConnectionEnergy

TAKE ACTION TIP 50

BE DIRECTIONALLY CORRECT

"You don't have to be perfect, you just have to be directionally correct."

— Chad Dummermuth (DuPont Engineer)

EARLY IN MY career, I worked in Equity Sales broking European stocks to Institutional clients like hedge, pension and mutual funds. Shortly after joining a new investment bank, I noticed that as soon as our morning sales call finished, the same guy (not by coincidence the top salesperson) was always the first one on the phone to clients. What I also noticed (he liked to be heard) was that, more often than not, what he was saying wasn't 100% accurate – but it was almost always **"directionally correct."** While the rest of us pondered how to perfect our pitches, he got the glory of being the first broker to alert clients of breaking news. He was also often the first to "fail" or to be told how his call was wrong (by both clients and eavesdropping colleagues) – but this just enabled him to quickly "course correct" and to hone his next sales call to be even more persuasive.

From him, I learned the **importance of courage in success and how to "fail fast"** – the courage to face our fears and make mostly, sort-of, on-balance right decisions based on all the incomplete information we have access to. Although **we seek the comfort and clarity of a binary**

world of right/wrong, good/bad, with things happening in a linear, orderly sequence, this is, unfortunately, not how the world works. **Success stems from having the courage to abandon certainty and to take imperfect action** in a world of grey decisions that are "directionally correct."

Harvard Professor Valiant showed how **taking "probably approximately correct" action improved an organism's performance by incorporation of information gathered from the environment**...a bit like my former stockbroking colleague.

So, **Today's Take Action Tip is to summon the courage to be directionally correct.** Ask yourself:

- **The Cartesian Coordinates:** What *will* happen if I *do* this? What *will* happen if I *don't do* this? What *won't* happen if I *do* this? What *won't* happen if I *don't* do this?
- **What is your intuition telling you?**
- **What does "good enough" look like?**
- **What would your most courageous self say about your next action?**

And then listen!

So, where is perfectionism holding you back?

"True Courage is the abandonment of certainty."

— Brendon Burchard

ASK YOURSELF, "WHAT DECISION DO I NEED TO MAKE TODAY TO BE MORE JOYFUL, CONFIDENT AND FULLY ENGAGED?"

#Clarity #Productivity #Courage #MindEnergy

TAKE ACTION TIP 51

SPEND TIME ON WHAT MATTERS MOST

"The trouble is, you think you have time."

— Buddha

I T'S FUNNY HOW we often speak about Time as if it were a thing. "I must *make* time," "I don't *have* enough time," "Where has the time *gone?*" "Time *flies!*" And when we lose a loved one, sadly, time *runs out*, as it did in December 2016 for my dear mother-in-law after a long battle with kidney disease. RIP dear Hazel Treadgold. Time, however, is the one thing I will always remember about her. How she always had time for everyone – a deeply caring woman and a servant leader long before Jim Collins popularised the term in his book *Good to Great*. From Magistrate to worldwide President of the Mother's Union to grandmother extraordinaire, she was a master of time and serving others. Routinely, gently, warmly checking up on others.

We all have the same 24 hours but how we decide to spend it is what makes a life. It is all too easy to put off doing the things you love to a future time called "someday."

So, **Today's Take Action Tip is to reflect on how you** spend **your time.** Do you:

- do what you love?
- spend time with people who uplift you?
- prioritise your passions and purpose?
- make a positive contribution?

It's also helpful to understand what time of day to spend time on the things that matter most to you. Are you an early bird or night owl – or somewhat of a mix? When you do things can be just as important as what things you do: Email and administrative tasks are best done in the trough (mid-afternoon lull for most). Focused, heads-down work is best when you're in the peak. Work out if that is morning or evening for you.

If not, how are you going to make your time matter?

> *"Time is a created thing. To say, 'I don't have time' is like saying 'I don't want to."*
>
> — Lao Tzu

ASK YOURSELF, "WHAT IS THE ONE THING I AM GOING TO SPEND TIME ON TODAY THAT REALLY MATTERS TO ME?"

#Clarity #Productivity #MindEnergy #ConnectionEnergy

TAKE ACTION TIP 51

CREATE A CONFIDENCE BOOSTING RITUAL

"Self-confidence is the memory of success."

— David Storey

DON'T YOU WISH you had a button to push whenever you needed a little confidence booster, either personally or professionally?

The good news is, confidence is not genetic, and you do not have to be reliant on others to increase it. And, even if you believe that you are not very competent, not very smart, not very attractive, etc., there are plenty of things you can do quite quickly to boost it.

If you find you are confident in some situations but lacking in others, then **Today's Take Action Tip is to create a confidence boosting ritual.**

- **Flip through your brag book:** What's that? You ask. It's a notebook in which you write each week your successes – good decisions made, things achieved, fears faced, fun had, letters and emails of thanks received, bonuses earned, awards won, steps out of comfort zone taken, etc. Hold on to those memories of your successes so you can relive the buzz.

- **Open your body:** Do a "power pose," stretch, smile with teeth, do yoga, stand up straight. This increases testosterone (for confidence and energy) and lowers cortisol (stress hormone). Hunching, slouching, frowning, sitting for long periods of time, crossing your arms and legs, etc., has the opposite effect.

- **Speak slowly:** It can make a big difference in how others perceive you. A person in authority, with authority, speaks slowly. It shows confidence. A person who feels that he isn't worth listening to will speak quickly because he doesn't want to keep others waiting on something not worthy of listening to. Breathe from your belly and SLOOOW down. It will help you look and feel in control.

- **Listen to your confidence "Jam" list:** "We will rock you," "Shake it off," "Roar"? What would be on your list?

"You wouldn't worry so much about what others think of you if you realized how seldom they do."

— Eleanor Roosevelt

ASK YOURSELF, "WHAT IS THE ONE THING I AM GOING TO SPEND TIME ON TODAY THAT REALLY MATTERS TO ME?"

#Courage #Clarity #MindEnergy #MoveEnergy #SpaceEnergy

Bonus tip

Pause for Some Quiet

"Silence is the sleep that nourishes wisdom."

— Francis Bacon

IN A 2013 study published in the journal *Brain, Structure and Function,* researchers found (sort of by accident) that **mice that were exposed to two hours of silence per day** (the control group in the study) **developed new cells in the hippocampus,** the part of the brain associated with memory, emotion and learning. The newly generated cells became functioning neurons and integrated into the system. So, basically **you can grow your brain with silence!**

By contrast, in 2011, the World Health Organization concluded that the 340 million residents of Western **Europe lost a million years of healthy life annually because of noise.**

Apparently the 19th century philosopher Arthur Schopenhauer had already intuitively worked out the power of noise on the brain: "*I have long held the opinion that the amount of noise that anyone can bear undisturbed stands in inverse proportion to his mental capacity and therefore be regarded as a pretty fair measure of it.*"

With the smartphone revolution of the past decade, the tiny cracks of quiet inactivity in **our lives are ruthlessly being filled up with more stimulus and noise.** In this relentlessly noisy, always-on world of mass distraction it, therefore, "sounds" like seeking out some silence might be a good idea.

So, **Today's Take Action Tip is to get some peace and quiet.** To follow are some ideas to build in some productivity-enhancing, brain-boosting pockets of silence into your day:

- **Go to a yoga class** – A 60-min yoga session boosts anxiety-quelling GABA neurotransmitters by 27% and increases healthy grey brain matter associated with increased pain tolerance as well as improved memory and decision making.

- **Block out distracting sounds** – Try some noise cancelling headphones, ear plugs or an amazing white noise generator for your desktop.

- **Meditate** – Freedom from noise and goal-directed tasks allows the brain to rest quietly and integrate external and internal information into "a conscious workspace."

- **Book a conference room at work or go to your local library** – This might provide a bit of respite if your workspace is too noisy.

- **Go for a walk, in nature** – A study conducted by researchers at the University of Michigan found that taking group nature walks is associated with a whole host of mental health benefits, including decreased depression, improved well-being and mental health, and lower perceived stress.

So, what strategies will you use to create a blank sensory slate of silence today?

> *"Silence is not the absence of something but the presence of everything."*

— John Grossman

"You wouldn't worry so much about what others think of you if you realized how seldom they do."

— Eleanor Roosevelt

ASK YOURSELF, "WHEN AND WHERE CAN I FIND 10 MINUTES OF QUIET TODAY?"

#Productivity #Clarity #MindEnergy #MoveEnergy #SpaceEnergy

ABOUT THE AUTHOR

SUSAN TREADGOLD SUSAN Treadgold is a three-time Bestselling Author and Co-author including *Success University for Women*, *Success University for Women in Business* and *The High Performing Woman: 52 Take Action Tips for Greater Confidence, Energy and Impact.*

She is also an elite Certified High Performance Coach, founder of Treadgold Executive Development, award-winning speaker and transformational trainer.

She is passionate about creating sustainable peak performance and success for clients by helping them to act with greater clarity, courage and influence in their careers, health and relationships and with increased confidence, energy and impact.

In addition to one-to-one coaching, she has created a Best Year Ever program for women in business, bespoke workshops/speeches, an annual De-Stress and Assess retreat, and a series of corporate career masterclasses.

Her international client list includes Barclays Bank, Expedia, Jefferies, JP Morgan, Man Group, Deutsche Bank, InvescoPerpetual and many high performing individuals.

Earlier in her career, she spent nearly two decades in senior Institutional Equity roles at investment banks DLJ, Morgan Stanley, Merrill Lynch and Citigroup.

She is based in San Diego and London and is a mother of two children, Rex and Cora.

Website: www.TEDlondon.com
Facebook: https://www.facebook.com/TreadgoldExecutiveDevelopment/
Twitter: @takeactionsusan
Linked-in: https://www.linkedin.com/in/susantreadgold
Amazon Author Page: https://www.amazon.com/Susan-Treadgold/e/B015NF4FIE

OTHER CO-AUTHORED BOOKS
BY SUSAN TREADGOLD

Success University for Women

Success University for Women in Business

Available on Amazon

Hire Susan To Speak at Your Event!

Book Susan Treadgold as your Keynote Speaker and You're Guaranteed to Make Your Event Highly Entertaining and Unforgettable!

F OR OVER A decade, Susan Treadgold has been coaching, educating, training and entertaining companies, teams and individuals to help get them to the next level of performance.

Her unique style inspires, empowers and entertains audiences while giving them the tools and strategies they need and want to have greater energy and success.

For more info, go to www.TEDlondon.com or send an email to admin@TEDlondon.

THE HIGH PERFORMING WOMAN'S PRAYER

Give me purpose, give me grace
Erase those stress lines from my face

Give me love and mindful connection
Loyal relationships and true affection

Give me work where I can create meaning
Serving others, together succeeding

Give me the courage to live my values
Hiding, conforming is not what I choose

Inspire me to action without endless reflection
Finding peace with perfect imperfection

Let me nourish my body, mind and soul
It's my health, I know that I'm in control

Help me to choose wise acts with intention
Instead of reacting and creating more tension

Let me be, all that I can be
not in my masculine, but authentically

Give me my confidence, give me my power
This is my time, this is my hour

Help me to create a vision to inspire me
And then to manifest it with infinite energy

ONE LAST THING...

I F YOU ENJOYED this book or found it useful, I'd be very grateful if you'd post a short review on Amazon. Your support really does make a difference and I read all the reviews personally, so I can get your feedback and make this book even better.

If you'd like to leave a review, then all you need to do is click the review link on this book's page on Amazon here:

https://www.amazon.com/High-Performing-Woman-Greater-Confidence-ebook/dp/B0786YY6LG/ref=la_B015NF4FIE_1_2?s=books&ie=UTF8&qid=1519940023&sr=1-2

Thanks again for your support!Enat. Furnicitilin dum, nimuntius, no. Otere, si publiis vid ato nos vessus consimus noxim ius vis.

Nostribus imil vit; ex nerum constanum co C. Abusserur latrate ia se cupioc, us nonsissigit, quod senatus, quem peri publicates essed fectus, consuamdium ur la L. Es horetimis? It predint? Duci sen vivius efenis. Misquonsit, sulesil nescerios, moensum, senium ta screst fitus cones M. Valicip teatum que prac menimor in dituam stiensuli sciermili, tam ocrestrum, Ti. es cus, orterfi castia patilis inatatu medit; Catuissimis, nocchus esse publi potinterox se coenatatis. C. Etra re prae inemed consult orendam es viritrid ceps, verita restate scivenducto adduciena, se ca nonverei fauraequam vercem que prehebendi publine moltumus; hororis.

Evirmiu sulabes terferis. Si sus in prius, quid ceri se novermi straverfent, Caturobunum hacrem, quam inpris.

Pos, scretebem acciordit, no. Nihilintem in se ad cursum escrum, est publica perurestor quam que pultis a dertati casta, ciam potifecto publiis prox mant. O ter ina, sentravemor inicerevive, eo, fuidem que

Made in the
USA
Lexington, KY